Praise for Gabrielle Bernstein

"I love Gabby and her work. She just has a special way of reaching people, and I *know* this book will change the shape of many hearts."

—India.Arie, singer, songwriter, and teacher

"I absolutely love *The Universe Has Your Back*. What makes it so incredibly special is Gabby's honesty about difficult experiences and how she learned and healed from them. By sharing these deeply personal stories, she allows us to feel that our own failures and shame can be brought into the light. This book is a refreshing and soul-nourishing read that I will go back to again and again."

—Rachel Platten, musician

"A new role model."

—*The New York Times*

"I came to one of Bernstein's monthly lectures and got my first look at the woman I'd one day unabashedly refer to as 'my guru.'"

—*ELLE* magazine

Featured on Oprah's Super Soul Sunday
as a next-generation thought leader

THE UNIVERSE HAS YOUR BACK

Transform Fear to Faith

GABRIELLE BERNSTEIN

HAY HOUSE, INC.

Carlsbad, California • New York City

London • Sydney • New Delhi

The Library of Congress has cataloged the earlier edition as follows:

Names: Bernstein, Gabrielle, author.
Title: The universe has your back : transform fear to faith / Gabrielle
  Bernstein.
Description: 1st Edition. | Carlsbad, California : Hay House, Inc., 2016.
Identifiers: LCCN 2016020275 | ISBN 9781401946548 (hardback)
Subjects: LCSH: Self-actualization (Psychology) | Fear. | Faith. | BISAC:
  SELF-HELP / General. | SELF-HELP / Personal Growth / Success.
Classification: LCC BF637.S4 .B475 2016 | DDC 204--dc23 LC record
available at https://lccn.loc.gov/2016020275

Tradepaper ISBN: 978-1-4019-4655-5
E-book ISBN: 978-1-4019-5201-3
Audiobook ISBN: 978-1-4019-5243-3

10 9 8 7 6 5 4 3 2 1
1st edition, September 2016
2nd edition, December 2018

Printed in the United States of America

For my dearest friend Micaela, thank you
for being my spiritual running buddy.

CONTENTS

INTRODUCTION

In the spring of 2015, I had a meltdown in a yoga class. Out of the blue, while in the middle of a sun salutation, I was taken over by terror and anxiety. I sat down on my mat to take a breath. It was then that I began to feel terrible pain in my neck, and the entire left side of my face and arm went numb. I started to freak out. I left the class, called my husband, and scheduled an emergency appointment with a doctor.

Within 24 hours I had undergone multiple MRIs and blood tests. Waiting for the results to come back was one of the scariest times of my life.

When the results did come back, I was at a loss. There was no diagnosis for my physical symptoms, and, ultimately, the doctors diagnosed the episode as a panic attack. This experience, however, seemed to make no sense. At this point in my life, I had an amazing and supportive husband, a thriving career, a healthy body, and a loving family. In fact, I was living a life far beyond my wildest dreams. I had spent a decade growing my spiritual practice, healing old wounds, and deepening my faith. And I was finally free—or so I thought.

In the following week, I managed to pull myself together, but I was still deeply concerned about why this had happened. My logical mind couldn't figure out what went wrong, so I turned to my meditation cushion for inner wisdom and guidance. Coming out of deep silence, I began to write in my journal. Words fell onto the page: "This is your resistance to love and freedom. The lingering darkness within you is resisting happiness."

I was taken aback by what I had written. Could all of this serious physical pain really be my resistance to love? For years I thought that once I worked through my past wounds, I'd be happy and free. Once I established a sense of security, I'd be happy and free. And once I had deepened my spiritual connection, I'd be happy and free. Through my commitment to my personal growth and my spiritual path, happiness and freedom did set in. My outside world began to reflect my positive internal condition, and life began to flow beautifully. And then, like clockwork, the presence of fear within me did everything it could to resist the love and light I had grown to rely on.

I looked closely at this resistance in order to understand and acknowledge its presence. After a lot of exploration, I came to understand that it's our resistance to love that keeps us in the dark. This resistance is the reason we stay stuck in patterns that keep us from thriving. You may have found that you regularly experience relief with meditation, prayer, positive affirmations, therapy, or any other type of personal growth, only to sabotage that great feeling with a limiting belief, negative comment, or addictive pattern. This experience continues to occur because the moment we lean toward the light, the darkness within us resists it.

Even when we make a commitment to love and happiness, we often find it hard to give up the fear we've grown to depend on. We give purpose to our pain, believing struggle and strife are necessary to success or lasting joy or a meaningful life, and we feel safe in a state of conflict and control. We carry an unconscious belief that in order to stay alive, we must hold on to our protection mechanisms, no matter how great love may feel.

You may be doing all you can to create freedom, connect to flow, and release your fear-based habits, but it's likely that the moment you feel some sense of relief, you're blindsided by the shadow of fear that dwells below the surface. You may not have recognized this pattern before, but when you do, you can begin the journey toward freedom. That's because the primary reason for our unhappiness is startlingly simple: *we are resistant to being happy.*

Sigmund Freud picked up on the phenomenon of resistance when many of his patients were not getting better. One night in a dream, it came to him that one of his patients wasn't improving because the patient did not want to improve. This dream led him to dedicate much of his practice to analyzing that resistance, which became a cornerstone of his treatment.

Unlike Freud's patient, you made a commitment to awaken from fear and get in sync with love the moment you opened this book. This commitment is massive. However, the presence of fear within you will do whatever it takes to keep you stuck in pain and darkness. This fear is the root cause of all our problems and feelings of disconnect. To truly say yes to the love of the Universe means you have to look at your resistance and give up a thought system that you mistakenly identified as safety, security, and the foundation of your life.

UNIVERSAL LESSON: TO BE FREE WE MUST ACKNOWLEDGE OUR RESISTANCE.

We must recognize that while we have a loving miracle mind-set within us that wants to be at peace, we also have a wrong mind that says, "I don't want to be free. I don't want to give up judgment. I don't want to release control."

The most profound way to practice releasing resistance is to see clearly how we don't want to let it go. When we accept that we are addicted to fear, we can let ourselves off the hook for anything that occurred in the past and for the detours into fear we will continue to make on our spiritual paths. We can forgive ourselves for not doing things perfectly, and we can forgive ourselves for holding on to old patterns. Honoring this shadow side of ourselves is the way to heal our resistance. The metaphysical text *A Course in Miracles* says, "We must not seek for the meaning of love but instead seek to remove all the barriers to love's presence."

In my case the moment that I accepted my fear was the moment my panic subsided. By embracing my fear and surrendering my desire to be free, an even greater pathway to freedom opened up to me. Today I no longer resist love, and I have faith that the loving energy of the Universe is available to me all the time.

You too can have this freedom. As you embark on the healing prayers, practices, and meditations in this book, what will serve you most is to look at your fear with love and decide that it's not a thought system you want anymore. Making this decision will clear the path to happiness.

Releasing your old thought system and welcoming in a new one takes practice, but it's a lot less "work" than you may think. The practice that will serve your highest good is the practice of surrendering to the love of the Universe. Each chapter in this book will give you simple prayers, affirmations, and exercises that support you in surrendering your fearful thoughts and energy to the right mind's grace. It's important that you don't overthink each practice. Just do it. You may find one or two practices that really resonate with you, and you may choose to repeat them more often. The perfect pathway will become clear, and you will map out the journey. However, rather than keep you on a specific plan or load you up with tools, I chose to present you with guidance that simply reminds you of what you long for most: freedom from fear so you can return to peace. The more you're reminded of what you want, the more you'll embrace your capacity to receive it.

The practice of being on a spiritual path isn't about being the best meditator, or the kindest possible person, or the most enlightened. The practice is about surrendering to love as often as possible. That's the goal of this book.

There are many exercises throughout this book. You may choose to practice them all, or you may fall in love with a few in particular. There's no right or wrong way to apply them. Just stay open and repeat the exercises that inspire you. If you apply just one lesson, prayer, or meditation from this book on a daily basis, you will experience a deeper connection to the Universe that will result in miraculous change. So keep it simple and know that the more you put in, the more you'll get out. As they say in the 12 Step communities, "It works if you work it."

So I ask you today to embrace your resistance, forgive yourself for being inconsistent with your practice (or for not having a practice at all), and surrender to the guidance that is before you. Begin each chapter with an open mind, and you will receive what you need. All that's required is your willingness to release whatever blocks you from living in harmony with the energy of love. As you turn the page, remember to remain open to new ideas; be patient and trust that the Universe has your back.

chapter 1

YOU HAVE A
HIDDEN POWER

When I was 16 years old, I struggled with depression. At the time I didn't know why I was depressed, but my feelings of fear, anxiety, and sadness were undeniable. My depression was sneaky; it showed up out of nowhere and seemingly without reason. Unable to rid myself of this problem, I turned to my mother for guidance. My mom—a hippie, meditator, and yogi—shared the tool she believed in: meditation. She sat me down on a meditation pillow and said, "This is the way out."

My mother taught me her mantra: *So, Ham, So, Ham.* And she suggested that I sit in meditation for at least five minutes a day to experience relief from depression. I was so stuck in sadness that I would have done whatever she said, and so I started my meditation practice. To my surprise, I instantly felt a sense of relief. This immediate gratification kept me coming back to my meditation pillow for more.

Two weeks into my practice, I took a weekend trip to a beach house with my boyfriend. The moment we arrived, the old feelings of depression and fear began to wash over me. I turned to my boyfriend and said, "I'm sorry, but I have to excuse myself to meditate." Then I walked up to a small room on the second floor of a home I'd never been in before. I sat in the dark on the neatly made bed and began my mantra: *So, Ham, So, Ham.* I had no idea what the mantra meant, but I knew it made me feel better. *So, Ham, So, Ham.* Within a minute of breathing and reciting the mantra, something miraculous happened. Out of nowhere I felt a warm blanket of loving energy wrap around me. My extremities began to tingle, and my anxiety and depression lifted. It was the greatest peace I'd ever experienced. I was in tune with a presence far greater than anything I'd ever known. I'd found my hidden power.

I remember this experience as if it were yesterday. It was the moment I realized I had the power to connect to a loving force of energy far beyond my logical mind and my physical site. It was the first time in my life that I felt truly safe. I walked out of the guest room and down the stairs to reunite with my boyfriend. My energy was lighter, my eyes were soft, and my spirit was rejuvenated. He looked at me and said, "What happened to you? You seem so clear." I replied, "Meditation."

I was diligent about my meditation practice for several months. But once I was feeling better, I began to slack. I started to get hooked into the safety, power, and excitement of outer successes and worldly forms of happiness. I turned to romantic relationships for safety and love. I turned to my career for a sense of accomplishment and satisfaction. And I turned to drugs to access that high I once found on my meditation pillow. I chose the outside world as my source of love and turned my back on the energy of the Universe.

Through a series of wrong-minded decisions to seek my safety outside myself, I plummeted to a dark bottom. I found myself once again in a deep depression, but this time it was amplified by addiction and shame. Then one morning as I sat on the floor of my apartment, coming down from drugs and alcohol, I called on that energetic connection I once had known. I turned to my mother's mantra, and I began to recite, *So, Ham, So, Ham, So, Ham.* As though no time had passed, I was instantly reunited with that feeling of love. It was as if invisible angel wings picked me up off that floor to help me step into a new way of living far beyond the fear I had chosen. Once again, I found my way out.

I made a commitment on that day—a commitment to never turn my back on the true source of love ever again. For the past decade, I've been on a spiritual journey of strengthening my relationship to that love. This love I speak of is known to many as God, spirit, truth, or consciousness. In our modern-day lexicon, many refer to it as "the Universe." Throughout the book I'll use these words interchangeably.

My relationship to this energy is the most important thing in my life. Without it I lose my power, my purpose, and my connection to love. Each day I devote to tuning in to this presence of love through prayer, meditation, mindful practices, and loving connections to myself and others. I take responsibility for the world I create by making love a habit, and I nurture the connection on a daily basis. That's why, even after decades of being a spiritual student, I still have to lean toward love each and every day. This is a commitment that I've made for a lifetime. And the good news is that it gets much easier. Like any new habit, the more you practice it, the more fun it becomes. Today I have an awesome relationship to the Universe, which, in turn, never lets me down.

UNIVERSAL LESSON: OUR HAPPINESS, SUCCESS, AND SAFETY CAN BE MEASURED BY OUR GENUINE CAPACITY TO TUNE IN TO THE LOVING VIBRATION OF THE UNIVERSE.

The reason so many people feel unhappy, unsuccessful, and unsafe is they forgot where their true happiness, success, and safety lie. Remembering where your true power lies reunites you with the Universe so that you can truly enjoy the miracles of life. And, most important, so your happiness can be an expression of joy that elevates the world.

Joy is our birthright. What blocks our joy is our separation from love. The way back to love begins with understanding how we disconnected in the first place. We all disconnect in our own unique ways. In some way or another, we deny the love of the Universe and choose the fear of the world. We choose to hook into the fears on the news, the fears in our classrooms, the fears in our households. We separate from the love of the Universe by giving purpose to pain and thinking power comes from outside sources. We deny the power of love, and we save our faith for fear. We forget love altogether.

The metaphysical text *A Course in Miracles* teaches, "The presence of fear is a sure sign you are trusting in your own strength." This is a profound message, and I remember gasping out loud when I first read it. *Separating from love* means that you deny the presence of a higher power (the presence of the Universe) and learn to rely on your own power to feel safe. The moment you choose to disconnect from the loving presence of the Universe, you lose sight of the safety, security, and clear guidance that is otherwise available to you. The moment you realign with love and stop relying on your own strength, clear direction will be presented. The presence of love will always cast out fear.

Being in union with the energy of the Universe is like an awesome dance where you trust your partner so much that you just surrender to the beat of the music. When you begin to dance with the energy of the Universe, your life flows naturally, incredible synchronicity presents itself, creative solutions abound, and you experience freedom.

My friend Carla is a great example of what happens when you realign with the presence of the Universe. Carla grew up in a family that rewarded outside success above all else and believed that one should do whatever it takes to achieve. As a result, she had a deep-rooted belief that relentless striving, stress, and struggle equaled success. She spent a decade building a high-powered career through a lot of pushing, controlling, and manipulating of outcomes. She believed that the harder she pushed, the more successful, happy, and safe she'd be. Her hard-driving energy led her to create a career that was very impressive outwardly. Then one day, at the top of her game, Carla had a nervous breakdown, and everything fell apart. She was rushed to the emergency room and was forced to go on disability to recover. The world as she knew it was over.

In the midst of her recovery, something happened to Carla that changed her life forever. One morning she woke up and lay still in her bed. In that stillness she remembered a prayer that her grandmother had taught her as a child. It was the prayer of Saint Francis of Assisi:

Lord, make me an instrument of thy peace!
That where there is hatred, I may bring love.

That where there is wrong, I may bring the spirit
of forgiveness.

That where there is discord, I may
bring harmony.

That where there is error, I may bring truth.

That where there is doubt, I may bring faith.

That where there is despair, I may bring hope.

That where there are shadows,
I may bring light.

That where there is sadness, I may bring joy.

Lord, grant that I may seek rather to comfort,
than to be comforted.

To understand, than to be understood.

To love, than to be loved.

For it is by self-forgetting that one finds.

It is by forgiving that one is forgiven.

It is by dying that one awakens to Eternal Life.

For whatever reason she felt guided to say this prayer out loud. Then she got out of bed and went on with her day. Although the day started off normal, as the hours went on things got wild. She sat down at her computer and an e-mail popped up on her screen. The e-mail was a link to a blog I had written; it was being forwarded to her from a friend she hadn't spoken to in years. The subject line was "Success is an inside job." The subject got Carla's attention. She opened the e-mail and clicked through to a video blog on my website, where I was offering tips for accessing success through spiritual practices. Carla still had no clue why she'd received this e-mail, who I was, or even why she'd clicked through to my site. All she knew was that an undeniable voice within her was yelling, "Watch that video!"

Carla watched the video and felt as though I were speaking directly to her. The next day she was in a bookstore, looking for a novel, when out of the blue a nonfiction book landed on the floor in front of her. It was my book *May Cause Miracles*. She recognized my face on the cover and laughed at the synchronicity. She couldn't deny this moment, so she bought the book and immediately began the 40-day practice.

Thirty days into the practice, Carla was cruising Facebook when a post from me popped up on her screen. The post stated that I was coming to her city to speak in two weeks. Carla bought her ticket instantly.

Carla attended the event, and she sat quietly in her seat when it came time for the Q&A. She had no interest in being seen or heard, especially as this self-help stuff was still new to her. Then I asked, "Who in this room has completed their 40-day practice of *May Cause Miracles*?" In that moment Carla realized that it was her 40th day! Involuntarily her hand rose up in the air, at which point I invited her to stand and share her experience. Carla began to share how she had no idea how that original e-mail made its way to her in-box or how the book fell off the shelf or how the Facebook ad landed on her screen 10 days before I arrived in her town. She went on to say that through her journey with the book, she had been guided to accept that her old way of living was no longer working. She had been guided to make new choices. She announced to a room full of strangers that she was quitting her high-stress job and going back to school to study nutrition, a subject she'd always longed to learn. She said, "Forty days ago I was deeply depressed, and today I know, as you say, that the Universe has my back."

Carla's story reminds us that when we surrender to the power of the Universe, we will always be guided to exactly what we need. The moment she said the Saint Francis prayer was the moment she stopped relying on her own strength and unconsciously asked the Universe for help.

Synchronicity, guidance, healing, and abundance are available to us *all the time*. All we need to do is tune in to the energy of the Universe so that we can get into the flow with the supportive, loving energy. When we're in alignment with this energy, life becomes a happy dream.

UNIVERSAL LESSON: WHEN WE SURRENDER OUR WILL TO THE POWER OF THE UNIVERSE, WE RECEIVE MIRACLES.

Another way to surrender to the power of the Universe is to get clear about how the stories and beliefs we carry dictate our experiences.

A Course in Miracles teaches us that *projection is perception*. This means that whatever stories you're projecting in your mind are what you're perceiving in your life. I learned a beautiful metaphor for this principle from a great *Course* teacher named Gary Renard. Imagine you're in a theater watching a scary film. You're at that point in the movie when something really bad is about to happen. You know that if the leading character turns the corner, she will walk into a life-threatening situation. You're throwing popcorn at the screen and screaming,

"Don't do it! Don't turn the corner!" Gary suggests that we think of this as the way we live our own lives. We're watching the movie screen that is our life, and we're screaming, "Don't go back to that relationship! Don't take that awful job! Don't pick up that drink!" But time and time again, we get stuck in the same horror scene.

Our projection is our perception. Here's a powerful example of how an old fearful story line, one I thought I'd healed, crept back in decades later.

In high school I was never part of a clique. I had a lot of funky guy friends who played in bands and smoked pot in their parents' basements. I loved these guys, but I always felt like an outsider because I didn't have a group of girlfriends. This experience led me to design an internal story line that I projected onto my life. My projection was that I was an outsider, and I'd never have a group of girlfriends. This projection became my perception for many years.

Then, in my mid-20s, I started leading workshops and lectures for large groups of women. Over time I had hundreds of women coming out to hang with me. The story began to heal, and I accepted that I was part of a power posse of like-minded women who shared my Spirit Junkie mentality.

Just when I was certain I'd healed my old fear perception, I came to realize that I wasn't fully free from that story line. The thing is, our fear stories are sneaky. They live in our psyches and our cells; they linger in our subconscious. Right when we think we're healed of the false projection, BAM! Something simple can trigger us and send us right back to the old fear. At this point in my life, I had many girlfriends and felt secure in my connections. However, there was one friend in my crew with whom

I never fully connected. She was always kind but never particularly warm or authentic. Something about her personality triggered my old fear story. Each year she invited all of us to a big party. A month before the invites typically went out, my fear story kicked in. I started to think that I wouldn't be invited to the party. I mentioned it to my husband, my friends, and anyone who would listen. My inner dialogue was, *The invites are going to go out, and I won't be invited.* Then, just as I'd expected, the e-mail invites went out and I didn't get one! I was deeply saddened. All my teenage feelings of being left out bubbled to the surface. I was angry and upset.

This led me into a tailspin. I went around telling my friends how upset I was that she didn't invite me to her party. I was an adult acting like a child. One morning I woke up very depressed. The first thought that came to mind was, *I'm not good enough. I'm an outsider.* Thankfully I had enough spiritual awareness at that point in my life that I was able to witness the story and choose to see it differently. I said out loud to myself, "Thank you, Universe, for helping me heal this. I forgive this thought, and I choose to see love instead." Then I went on with my day.

Later that afternoon I had lunch with a friend. I mentioned to him that I hadn't been invited to the party. He laughed out loud and said, "What, are you nuts? Of course you were invited! Just text her and see what happened." Because I had said my prayer earlier that morning, I was humbled enough to hear his suggestion. An involuntary response came out of me: "Okay, I'll text her." I picked up my phone and sent a message, "Hey how are you? I didn't receive the invite to your party. I hope everything is okay between us." Within seconds she replied, "What?! Of course you were invited!

I sent the e-mail from a new account so make sure to check your spam filters." I checked my spam filter, and of course . . . the invite was there.

This story clearly outlines how our projection creates our perception. Because I was so caught up in the story that I was an outsider and not invited, I wasn't open to the possibility that the e-mail could be in my spam box. This was such an obvious scenario, considering how all my e-mails get filtered these days. But because I was so stuck in the story, I cut off my connection to loving possibilities and had committed to fear.

Energy flows where your attention goes. My focus and attention had been so negative that I cut off the possibility for love. Then the moment I said my prayer, I opened up my consciousness to receive new information. This was my way out of the fearful projection.

The good news is that the way out of our fear projections is simple. Gary, the *Course* teacher with the spot-on movie-theater metaphor, suggests that we consider what would happen if we just walked back into the projection room and changed the reel. What would happen if we changed our projection? What would we perceive?

UNIVERSAL LESSON: YOU SEE THE WORLD THAT YOU HAVE MADE, BUT YOU DO NOT SEE YOURSELF AS THE IMAGE-MAKER.

There are a few steps you can take to remembering your hidden power.

Step 1: What is the fearful movie you've been playing?

Using Gary's metaphor, take a moment to contemplate the idea that you are the director of the movie that

is your life. Think about the movie you've been projecting onto your own life and contemplate the following:

- What fear-based stories from the past or
  projections about the future are you playing
  on your internal movie screen?

- How are these stories blocking you from
  feeling supported and happy?

Step 2: What's the positive movie you've been playing?

The same way the fearful stories block you from the
flow of the Universe, your positive stories empower your
life. Let's look closely at the powerful stories you're replay-
ing on your internal projector. (Note: You may be stuck
in a lot of fear right now and may have trouble finding
an empowering story. Just keep it simple. An empowering
story can be, *I feel happy and connected when I'm cooking.
Or I'm in the flow with the Universe when I'm on a long run.*)

- What are the love-based empowering stories
  that you replay in your head?

- How do these stories make you feel
  supported and happy?

This exercise will help you understand how the
positive projections you believe in are supporting your
connection to the Universe and how your negative projections are keeping you stuck. A big goal throughout
this book is to bring more energy to the positive stories
and use the forthcoming practices to help you heal the
negative ones.

UNIVERSAL LESSON: LOOK FOR LOVE IN ALL THE RIGHT PLACES.

Step 3: Reconnect to your power.

When you focus on the positive stories, you raise your energy, elevate your presence, and even boost your immune system to keep you feeling physically strong. Positive stories make you feel good. In the presence of feeling good, you are powerful. Your presence is your power. When your internal movie screen is projecting an empowering story, then your perception of your life is empowered. When you dwell in an energy of positivity and power, you become a magnet for miracles.

I can easily describe to you what it feels like to be connected to the power of my presence. When I'm aligned with my presence, I'm breathing easily, words come to me without overthinking, I feel genuinely confident, and people resonate with my energy. I feel safe, calm, and in the flow with whatever is happening around me. When I'm out of alignment with the power of my presence, I feel stuck, weak, tired, anxious, and annoyed. No one wants to be around me, and I feel disconnected from everyone. It's invaluable for me to clearly know the difference between what it feels like to be connected to my presence versus what it feels like when I'm not. This awareness helps me witness when I'm out of alignment so I can choose to realign in an instant.

Throughout this book I will guide you to proactively fine-tune your presence with a ton of powerful tools that will keep you connected. Let's begin now by raising your awareness of what it feels like to be in that energy and how the outside world responds to your inner power.

Take a moment to answer these questions.

What does it feel like when I'm connected to the presence of my power?

What does it feel like when I'm disconnected from my power?

Become very aware of what it feels like to be aligned with your power versus what it feels like to be disconnected. This awareness is the most crucial step to reconnecting with your hidden power.

The way back to your power is simple. Whenever you notice yourself disconnect from the presence of love, simply say this prayer to come back to peace, "I witness that I'm out of alignment with my power. I choose to see peace instead of this."

This prayer will reconnect you to your desire to be in union with your creative power. Your desire is enough to help you begin to reconnect. Make the conscious commitment to realign with your power, and you will begin to feel the shift set in.

UNIVERSAL LESSON: YOUR PRESENCE IS YOUR POWER.

After one of my lectures, an audience member asked me, "Are you connected to your power presence all the time?" I quickly responded, "Heck no! I get taken out all the time. But I know how to come back quickly." Restoring your energy and your power presence is as easy as Gary's metaphor: The moment you notice yourself disconnected from the feeling of your power, you can change the reel. Through the power of your intentions you can reorganize your energy *in an instant*. Remember that your intentions create your reality.

Power lies in knowing how your positive presence expands your outer life. With this newfound awareness, you can easily see when you're in alignment with your power and when you're not. When you're disconnected, you can recite your prayer and get back into the flow.

I witness that I'm out of alignment with my power. I choose to see peace instead of this.

This prayer will always realign you with the power you have to return to love. In any given moment, you can choose again. The practice of choosing again will help you stay connected to the Universe. Your simple intention to choose again will bring your power out of hiding and restore your presence.

The simplest shifts can reconnect you in an instant. As you get into the practice of mindfully making these shifts, you'll in turn begin to experience love, flow, synchronicity, and a tremendous amount of guidance. Take these Universal lessons seriously, and your high-vibe energy will clear the path for a life beyond your wildest dreams.

- Meditation and prayer open you up to the power of the Universe.

- The presence of fear shows up when you're not relying on the Universe.

- Your projection is your perception. Become aware of the fear-based stories you've been projecting on your internal movie screen.

- Your presence is your power. Be mindful of how your thoughts, words, and energy disconnect you from the Universe. And know the difference between what it feels like to be connected to the presence of your power versus what it feels like when you're not.

- When you notice yourself disconnect from the presence of love, say this prayer to come back to peace: "I witness that I'm out of alignment with my power. I choose to see peace instead of this."

In the next chapter, we go deeper on the power of your thoughts and energy. I help you become more aware of how your intentions create your reality. This work can feel a bit overwhelming at first. Taking responsibility for the world we've created can seem scary. But remember, you can choose how you want to perceive every situation in your life, including your healing process. Let's set the intention to move into the next chapter with enthusiasm for your journey and a desire to expand your inner awareness with self-forgiveness and grace. This process is meant to be joyful. Let yourself off the hook, and surrender to the guidance you're receiving. Have fun!

chapter 2

YOU ARE THE DREAMER OF YOUR DREAM

What we focus on we create—be it good or bad. As we learned in Chapter 1, the stories we project on our internal movie screens become the experiences we perceive to be our realities. We spend our days collecting information and images to support our inner movies. We are in a constant state of focusing on certain images and filtering out others. In doing so, we are actively choosing the world we perceive. The more attention we pay to certain images, the more we filter out others.

Lesson 21 of *A Course in Miracles* says, "I am responsible for what I see." This lesson reinforces the idea that our projection is our perception. The *Course* emphasizes that what we perceive is based solely on our interpretations. For instance, we can interpret a fight with our spouse as another reason to consider a divorce, or we can choose to see it as a powerful opportunity to learn and grow stronger as a couple. We can perceive a negative health diagnosis with complete terror or a chance to slow down and truly start embracing each moment with gratitude.

No matter how dire the circumstances, we can choose to perceive with love or with fear. Our own interpretation determines our perception of the reality we experience.

You may be thinking: That's all fine and nice for those of us living in developed, stable societies where we have food, safety, and other necessities (not to mention luxuries). But what about someone in a poor country or someone who's challenged by war or life-threatening circumstances? What about someone wrestling with poverty or other extreme circumstances? How does this person choose to perceive their world with love? While our individual circumstances may vary the degree of difficulty in practicing this exercise, there are numerous examples of the perseverance of the human condition through horrible situations. Consider Elie Wiesel, who turned his experience of the Holocaust into an existential journey that made him one of the greatest writers and healers of our time. Or Mahatma Gandhi, who chose peaceful protest in the midst of leading the Indian independence movement. Or Leymah Gbowee, who bore witness to the worst of humanity and helped bring Liberia out of a horrific civil war through women's leadership. What all these heroes share is a willingness to perceive their circumstances with love. Fear would have led them to violence and death. Love led them to rise above the perceptions of darkness and into the light.

UNIVERSAL LESSON: WE ARE NOT RESPONSIBLE FOR WHAT OUR EYES ARE SEEING. WE ARE RESPONSIBLE FOR HOW WE PERCEIVE WHAT WE ARE SEEING.

You don't have to be a world leader to have a radical shift in perception. Sometimes it can be as simple as choosing to perceive your job with more gratitude or your family with more love. A small shift can change you forever. In my own life, for years I perceived my body as weak because of how easily I got sick. I spoke of myself as having a poor constitution, and I set up a story that I was fragile. This perception of my body led me to be even more susceptible to illness.

Then in my mid-30s, I began planning for a family. At that point I knew I had to make a change. I wanted to create a baby in a healthy environment and clear any blocks to my capacity to get pregnant. I was also fed up with my old fear-based perception of my body. I became ready to change what I saw on my internal projection screen. I trusted that by changing my internal story, I'd be guided to new perceptions.

So I hit my knees and prayed for a new perception of my body. I prayed for guidance in whatever form it needed to come. Days later I got a call from my friend Michael. He said, "I got you an appointment with my naturopath, Dr. Linda. It's nearly impossible to get an appointment with her, but I felt strongly that you needed her support, so I put a call in." He went on to say, "I wasn't sure if I was going to be able to get you in, but then the most amazing thing happened. I mentioned your name to Dr. Linda's assistant, and she was happy to help. As it turns out, she has been following your work for years."

I was so blown away by Michael's generosity and the divine synchronicity that I graciously accepted. This guidance astonished me. You see, a few months prior to Michael's intervention (and a few months before I'd surrendered to my health), I'd heard of Dr. Linda through another friend and tried to get an appointment. Remember, at that time I hadn't fully surrendered to getting healthier. Each time I called her office and left a message, I didn't even get a response. I knew from my friends how hard it was to see her, and I believed them. So I gave up on Dr. Linda, assuming she was too busy for new patients. My apathy toward my health blocked me from getting an appointment. But the instant I became ready to change my perception of my body, Michael got the Universal memo and intervened.

UNIVERSAL LESSON: THE UNIVERSE WILL ALWAYS CONSPIRE TO LEAD YOU TOWARD SOLUTIONS OF THE HIGHEST GOOD WHEN YOU OPEN UP TO RECEIVE THEM.

The key to receiving spiritual guidance is to be open to it. My shift in perception about my body led me to receive the exact help I needed for a radical healing journey. Through Dr. Linda's counsel, I cleaned up my diet, removing sugar, yeast, dairy, and gluten. I began to take helpful supplements and cleanses. I became aware of how food, travel, and stress were affecting my body. This knowledge gave me power. I began to pray over all my homeopathic remedies and supplements. I'd infuse the power of positive energy into my medicine to amplify their effects on my body. I committed to a new internal story: *I am proactively healing my body. I am healthy and I am free.*

This healing process didn't come without challenges, but I felt a new sense of power. I had been guided to a solution of the highest good, and I was proud of myself for showing up for it. Even though my body didn't heal overnight, my perception of my body did just that. And my new perception gave me the energy and the conviction to stay on the path. This new story set me free from fear and opened me up to infinite possibilities for healing.

Today I have full faith in the way I treat my body, and I know that I am becoming stronger in each moment. I now perceive my old health challenges as a great teacher. I have transformed my perception of my body, and I've come to learn that my body is a vessel through which I spread love. And I feel superawesome!

UNIVERSAL LESSON: THE UNIVERSE IS OUR CLASSROOM, AND WHEN WE ACCEPT OUR ROLE AS THE HAPPY LEARNER, LIFE GETS REALLY GROOVY.

The moment I chose to see my health issues with a loving perspective, I was able to receive support from the Universe. The way we perceive our life's circumstances will determine how we respond to them. If we see our difficulties with lack, judgment, and fear, then we'll respond with lack, judgment, and fear, in effect blocking all guidance from the Universe. But when we choose to see the same issues with love, we create space for miracles.

In any given situation, we can choose the teacher of fear or we can choose the loving guidance of the Universe.

UNIVERSAL LESSON: WHEN WE CHOOSE THE UNIVERSE AS OUR TEACHER, WE CAN SEE WITH THE EYES OF LOVE.

Choosing the loving guidance of the Universe doesn't come naturally to us. We live in a fear-based world, and our default setting is to lean toward fear. The same way that we manifest love by aligning with the Universe, we manifest chaos when we align with fear. We're *always* manifesting either love or fear. It's up to us to decide how we want to create our reality.

Ending the cycle of manifesting fear is far simpler than you think. *A Course in Miracles* says:

Do not be concerned how you can learn a lesson so completely different from everything that you have taught yourselves. How would you know? Your part is very simple. You need only recognize that everything you learned you do not *want*. Ask to be *taught* and do not use your experiences to confirm what you have learned.

The following steps will begin your dialogue with the Universe. These will become the backbone of your spiritual practice. Throughout the book you'll be encouraged to call on them.

Step 1: Ask for guidance.

The moment you pray for guidance, you reconnect with your inner wisdom, the voice of love. In an instant you can release the teacher of fear and choose the teacher of love by welcoming spiritual guidance. Think of this spiritual connection as a loving friend, an intermediary, guiding your thoughts from fear to love.

That's how simple this is. Just ask for help.

Try it now.

Pick any area of your life that feels blocked.

Now ask for guidance: "Thank you, Universe, for guiding me to perceive this fear through the teacher of love."

Notice how you feel after saying this prayer. It's possible that you may have felt immediate relief. Continue to use this prayer throughout your day and pay attention to every moment of relief and the guidance that you receive. My hope is that this prayer process will help you see how easy it is to realign with the energy of the Universe and choose the perception of love. In any moment, no matter how far down the negative path of fear you've gone, you can choose again. You can always choose again.

Step 2: Practice the Holy Instant.

When you pray to learn through the teacher of love over the teacher of fear, you experience what *A Course in Miracles* calls the "Holy Instant." The Holy Instant is the moment that you surrender your fear to the care of the Universe and accept the perspective of love. It's not temporal, or based in time. Rather, it's an instant out of time and space in which our decision-making mind realizes it made a mistake (the "unholy instant") and invites the loving perception of the Universe to reinterpret the situation. The shift in perception enables us to understand that the world outside is a projection of the world we created in our mind; that *the problem is not outside, but within*. We're reminded that there's a loving spiritual presence that can restore us to sanity. That's the Holy Instant. And when we witness the Holy Instance, we experience a miracle.

Through your new prayer, you can practice the Holy Instant all the time. The more perceptual shifts you create, the more you will feel connected to the flow of the Universe. This practice is crucial as we move forward with the work in this book.

I recently witnessed a beautiful example of the Holy Instant in action. My friend was complaining about how much he despised his boss. He went on and on about how his boss led with an iron fist, constantly put everyone down, and created a negative work environment. My friend was angry and distraught about the situation, but (and this is crucial!) he was willing to see it differently. His willingness led him to say the magic words to me: "I need help. I want to see this differently." This request for help opened the invisible door to the Universal realm of spiritual guidance.

Spirit works through people, and on this day spirit worked through me. I responded to him by teaching him the Holy Instant. I explained to him that through the practice of turning your fear over to love, you could shift your perception of your enemy into the perception of a brother. Together we said a prayer. We said, "Thank you, spirit, for your guidance. We surrender this grievance to you, and we welcome you in to reorganize all limiting beliefs back to love."

Instantly my friend felt better. I could see the relief come over his face. We said our good-byes and accepted the miracle of the Holy Instant. Then an hour later I got a call from him. He said, "The coolest thing happened. When I got home, I stood in my hallway remembering what you said. I heard your voice say, 'Choose to see him as a brother.' Then I looked down at the mail in my hand, and at the top of the pile was a Christmas card from my boss. In that instant I felt a rush of love come over me, and I was able to see him as my brother. I felt connected to him in a different way. I forgave him and prayed for him to be happy this holiday season. Wow!" I responded, "This is the Holy Instant, my friend. It's available to you all the time."

Step 3: Fast comeback.

The Holy Instant is available to us all. We just have to choose it. The more we practice the Holy Instant, the faster we return to love.

UNIVERSAL LESSON: OUR HAPPINESS IS A DIRECT REFLECTION OF HOW QUICKLY WE CAN RESTORE OUR FEAR BACK TO LOVE.

This is what I call the comeback rate. How quickly can you come back to love? The world we perceive will give us countless opportunities to disconnect from love. All you have to do is turn on the news, step into a packed subway, or get stuck driving in traffic in order to feel hooked into negativity and fear. The miracle isn't how well we avoid fear; the miracle is how quickly we return to love.

Remember: the goal isn't to avoid fear. Fear will never go away altogether, and if you pour your energy into trying to avoid it, you miss the opportunity to experience the Holy Instant. Instead, the goal is to not believe in fear.

Commit to practicing the Holy Instant. Whenever you notice yourself stuck in the fear-based story, use your prayer: "Thank you, Universe, for guiding me to perceive this fear through the teacher of love."

Whenever we align our thoughts with love, we can truly feel the presence of the Universe behind us. As you begin to shift your perceptions out of fear, it's important to get clear about the world you want to see. Many folks can get hung up about this concept because even though they are willing to surrender fear, a deep-rooted feeling that they don't deserve love remains. This mentality blocks the capacity to step into the flow.

In every situation you have two choices: Will you learn through fear or will you learn through love?

UNIVERSAL LESSON: THE UNIVERSE IS ALWAYS RESPONDING TO THE ENERGY BEHIND YOUR BELIEFS.

Step 4: Put out what you want to receive.

Our energy transmits a message, and that message will always be supported. If you're aligned with a belief system of fear, then your experiences will be backed with fear. If you retrain yourself to choose love, then you'll experience life through the lens of love. It's not that your experiences change but that your experience of your experiences change.

A powerful example of this is a young woman named Samantha, whom I've worked with for five years. Samantha is a kick-ass copy editor, and she is one of the most amazing people I've ever employed. Not only is she fantastic at the work she produces but she's also lovely to collaborate with. Over the years we've become very close friends. This past year I sent Samantha a ton of work to do, and she always returned her assignments right on time. She never missed a beat. Oddly, Samantha would never bill me for all her work. Month after month I'd ask her to send me an invoice. She'd either ignore the e-mail or say, "I'll get to it when I'm less busy." This made me uncomfortable. I energetically felt her apathy toward getting paid and her fear of accepting abundance. I also wanted to honor her great work, and she was blocking the flow of abundance. I kept my mouth shut and trusted that the Universe was guiding her to learn an important lesson.

Then December rolled around, and we were nearing the New Year. I looked at my accounting and realized that I hadn't paid her one cent all year long. I immediately e-mailed her and said, "Sister, please let me pay you!"

Within moments she replied, "I'm working on the invoice FOR REAL this week. The Universe hit me over the head with the importance of getting paid—several clients have been taking their SWEET, SWEET TIME paying me (like months after I've submitted invoices), requiring almost aggressive follow-up. I took it as a sign. I'll send you an invoice this week. xx"

I replied, "Yes, that is a sign. If you don't receive money from clients who want to pay you, then you tell the Universe that you don't really want to get paid. Then the flaky clients pick up the Universal memo and DON'T PAY YOU. It's time to put out the message and the mantra, 'I GET PAID FOR MY AWESOME WORK. AND I GET PAID ON TIME!'"

In her final response she said, "Amen, Gabby. I really had to be knocked over the head to get that message."

Samantha's story reminds us that the energy we put out is what we will receive.

Take a moment to reflect on where you focus your energy. Are you projecting an attitude of apathy, stress, jealousy, or fear? Look closely at how what you focus on reflects back to you what you receive.

I hope this lesson helps you become conscious of the messages you're sending the Universe before they become a problem. Imagine what would happen if you changed your patterns before the Universe "knocked you over the head" with the lesson. What if you shifted your energy before the money was gone or before the marriage was broken or before the addiction had beaten you down? Why not get there sooner? When we choose to perceive the world with love, we can completely reorganize our experience of life. Accepting this truth can save you from years of tortured drama and pain.

So let's go there now. Do you want to learn through love, or do you want to learn through fear? In the next lesson, you'll make a commitment to the love of the Universe with a purpose statement.

Step 5: Create a purpose statement.

This is a statement to the Universe. Whenever you put pen to paper, you sign a sacred contract. You send a powerful message to the Universe that you're willing to surrender your fear and that you're ready to let love lead the way. Put it on the page, baby! This is a huge step in surrendering to the Universe. We cannot stop the learning process, but we can align with the energy of love to make it much more fun. Your purpose is to learn through love.

If you're ready to commit to learning through love, then state your purpose to the Universe. Write it down now on a piece of paper or in your journal: *I am ready to learn through love.*

When you make this type of commitment to the Universe, it's important to be aware of any sneaky, fear-based story that can hook you back in. This is the story that *pain has purpose.* We live in a world that supports drama, terror, separation, and hardship. We've been guided to believe that without pain we have not accomplished or achieved. I'm here to *bust that myth now.* Pain does not equal purpose. Your purpose is to be joyful. Your purpose is to live with ease. Your purpose is to surrender to the love of the Universe so you can live a happy life. Accept the purpose of love, and your life will radically change this instant.

Use your new purpose statement daily. When you wake up, say: *I am ready to learn through love.* When you come across a difficult situation or a negative thought, simply say: *I am ready to learn through love.* Make this your mantra.

Each moment that you invite the Universe to reinterpret your fear and transform it to love, you'll experience the Holy Instant. Keep practicing the Holy Instant so that your perceptions will begin to lean toward love naturally. Every word we say and every image we see symbolizes either love or fear. When the symbols we choose all begin to vibrate with love, then we feel much more supported by life. Take ownership of the symbols you choose by clarifying what you want to see.

Step 6: You are the dreamer of your dream.

You are the dreamer of your dream that is your life. At times your dream may feel like a nightmare if you've disconnected from the love of the Universe and instead identify with the fear of the world. When you rely on the spiritual guidance of the Universe, you'll be led out of the nightmare and into a happy dream. A dream of new perceptions that resembles the truth of who you are: love.

For this sacred moment, offer yourself the opportunity to do an exercise of image making. The images you focus on are the images that make up the dream that is your life. That's why this exercise is crucial to accepting that the Universe has your back.

UNIVERSAL LESSON: CREATE VISIONS OF THE WORLD YOU WANT TO SEE.

A Course in Miracles says, "The mind is very powerful, and never loses its creative force. It never sleeps. Every instant it is creating. It is hard to recognize that thought and belief combine into a power surge that can literally move mountains."

We must learn to train our minds to create with love rather than with fear. This exercise is a great practice for you to begin awakening to the power of your own creations.

Begin the practice of image making by answering this simple question: What do you want to see? Be unapologetic about your answer. Maybe you want to see a world without war. Maybe you want to see yourself in a wildly romantic relationship. Maybe you want to see yourself walking through life free from fear. Create the images you most long for.

Write down your answer now. What do you want to see?

Next, read your response and then close your eyes and sit in stillness for five minutes. You can follow the meditation here, or for further guidance you can use my image-making guided meditation, which you can find at www.gabbybernstein.com/universe.

Image-making meditation:

Sit up straight, resting your hands on your thighs with your palms facing upward. When you sit up straight with proper, natural (not stiff) alignment, you become a channel to receive positive energy.

Close your eyes and turn your focus inward.

Allow your inner spirit (your inspiration) to come forth and surrender to the images that you want to see.

Let the wisdom within you create images in your mind's eye.

Surrender to this wisdom now.

Breathe deeply in through your nose and out through your mouth.

With each inhale and exhale, surrender more fully to the visions that you want to see.

Consciously focus your attention on them.

Allow visions of what you want to guide you on a journey of new perceptions.

Sit as long as you wish.

When you're ready, gently come out of your meditation and take a moment to jot down any images that may have come through. Maybe what you want to see is a newborn baby, and in your meditation you saw the eyes of a child. Or maybe you long for a romantic partner, and in the stillness you saw yourself in a warm embrace with a lover. It's even possible that you saw images that were far less literal and in time you'll come to understand the message behind them.

UNIVERSAL LESSON: THE VISIONS YOU SEE IN STILLNESS OFFER YOU GREAT GUIDANCE AND REASSURANCE THAT YOU'RE BEING SUPPORTED.

If you didn't experience any imagery, maybe you had an emotional reaction or a shift in your energy.

Write down whatever happened.

This exercise is the beginning of opening the door to a collaboration with the energy of the Universe. When you humbly surrender through prayer and meditation, you begin to receive guidance far beyond your physical site. Often you'll feel a presence within you and around you, guiding your thoughts and feelings. Do not be afraid to dive deeply into the infinite pool of inner wisdom that is available to you now. Open your heart and mind to new perceptions. Allow yourself to surrender to the flow of love that always guides you. Most important, accept that you have the right to be happy. You have the right to thrive, shine, and succeed. Give yourself the gift of opening your mind to a world beyond what you have been taught to believe in. A world of infinite possibilities. A world of love.

Right now you have the chance to choose to let go of littleness, to choose the teacher of love, and to choose to see what you desire. In this instant you can experience the shift you have been longing for.

Make love your primary choice on a moment-to-moment basis. I know you may be thinking, *Well, that's all fun and nice, but what about when my boss is an ass or when I'm terrified by the news on TV?* My response to this is:

In the midst of the darkness, grab a flashlight.

The steps outlined in this chapter are the flashlights. The light is available to you at all times; all you have to do is turn it on by tuning in.

Let's recap the key steps from this chapter:

- Choose the teacher of love. Accept that you'd rather learn through love.

- Practice the Holy Instant and pray to learn through the teacher of love over the teacher of fear.

- Fast comeback. Remember, your happiness is a direct reflection of how quickly you can shift your fear to love.

- Align your thoughts with love. The Universe always responds to the energy behind your beliefs.

- Commit to your purpose statement: *I am ready to learn through love.*

- You are the dreamer of your dream. Create visions of the world you want to see.

Stay committed to these steps as we continue on our journey together. Each chapter will build on the next; each lesson you learn will support what's to come. The more you commit to these lessons, the more fun this book will be for you. Right now you have a choice to learn through joy. Let's go for it!

In Chapter 3 I help you understand how the Universe is always guiding you to heal your fear-based thoughts and images through divine Universal assignments. It will be your choice whether you want to show up for these assignments. But if you do, great healing will occur.

YOU ARE ALWAYS BEING GUIDED. *EVEN WHEN IT DOESN'T FEEL LIKE IT.*

As you journey further into the lessons in this book, it's helpful to keep in mind that the world is your classroom and other people are your assignments. Every experience you perceive on the movie screen that is your life gives rise to one of two choices: to learn through the perception of love or to learn through the perception of fear. Each instance is a holy encounter providing a divine spiritual assignment in which you can choose to heal or to stay stuck in the bondage of your past. If you choose to show up for these Universal assignments with a willingness to heal, then many miracles will be presented to you. But if you're unwilling to show up for these assignments, you will stay stuck in the stories and experiences that do not serve you.

A powerful example is my friend Lance. Growing up, Lance picked up a fear-based story that he wasn't smart enough. He went through his life trying to control this fear by anesthetizing his discomfort with alcohol, relationships, work, and all sorts of addictive behavior. Numbing his fear got him nowhere. In his early 30s, Lance wised up to the fact that he was avoiding his discomfort, and he made the powerful decision to get sober and begin a path of recovery.

I met Lance early in his recovery, and we became great friends. By this point I was coming up on 10 years of sobriety and was well aware of all the ways fear plays a role in early recovery. I was, therefore, able to witness Lance's experiences and help guide him to see the Universal lessons in his discomfort.

Two years into Lance's recovery, he got into a relationship with an awesome woman. This lady was great! She treated him well and respected his opinions. What was most interesting about this woman, although Lance couldn't see it at first, was that her sense of humor triggered all his insecurities. She would often joke with him about how he wasn't up to speed with the latest news or how he couldn't figure out how to follow a simple recipe. What was merely a joking way of pushing a lover's buttons majorly triggered Lance. Even though his girlfriend was kidding around and having fun, her jokes gave new life to Lance's old fear story of not being smart enough. Lance projected his old story onto his new experience, choosing to see through the lens of fear rather than the lens of love.

Lance came to me for advice, feeling deeply wounded and upset. He said, "I'm just going to have to break up with her. Clearly I'm not enough for her. She deserves someone smarter than me." I responded with a spiritual throw-down: "Hold up, man! This is your crazy talking. You're projecting your old fear story onto a totally innocent situation!" Within a few minutes, he was able to see clearly how he had projected the perception of fear onto his new girlfriend.

I went on to explain to Lance that this girlfriend was the perfect Universal assignment for him to face his fear. This woman was no accident: she was divinely placed in his life at a time when he was ready to heal his old wounds and recover once and for all. His commitment to get sober sent a message to the Universe that he was willing to play big in this lifetime and restore his faith in love. I explained that he'd unconsciously asked for greater healing and the Universe provided it—in the form of a loving woman who would push all his buttons so that he'd be forced to finally face his fear.

Lance resisted this concept at first. "It's too painful. I can't face it," he said. "She deserves someone better." I replied, "Are you willing to be happy and free?" He said, "Yes, of course." I responded, "Then you better show up for this assignment now, or it will just show up again and again in all your future partners." Lance took my advice and followed the steps I suggested for how to show up for his Universal assignment.

You too probably have a universal assignment waiting for you. Maybe it's a fearful story from the past that you projected onto the present. Or maybe, like Lance, you don't even realize there is anything to face. Perhaps you just assume that you are the victim of the world you see and that there is nothing you can do about it. Well, I'm here to bust that myth now. You are *not* a victim and you *can* be happy and free. If you're ready to begin the journey toward freedom, then it's time to show up for the Universal assignment.

UNIVERSAL LESSON: THE WORLD IS YOUR CLASSROOM, AND PEOPLE ARE YOUR ASSIGNMENTS.

Below are the steps I shared with Lance. Follow them to begin the process of showing up for your Universal assignments.

Step 1: Recognize the assignment and call it by its name.

The first step is to witness that what may seem to be a terribly uncomfortable situation is actually a Universal assignment. In other words, witness your craziness and call it by its name: fear. Then accept that the fear has shown up in this way as a divine assignment for healing and growth.

Take a deep, honest look at the situation that's causing you pain, and identify all the ways that the person or circumstance is triggering your fear-based beliefs. Honor yourself for having the strength to witness this instead of running from it. Be proud of yourself for seeing it as an assignment.

Trust that if you weren't ready to accept this assignment, you wouldn't have even opened this book! By choosing to read a book like this, you unconsciously signed a sacred contract that said you're ready to go big, you're ready to heal, and you're ready to be free.

Step 2: Accept that you cannot avoid the assignment.

The second step is all about accepting that you can't avoid the assignment—you can only postpone it. If you don't choose to accept the assignment today, it will continue to present itself in new relationships and experiences. If you don't show up for it, it will continue to show up for you.

You have two choices in this situation: The first choice is that you can follow FEAR—F Everything and Run. Sometimes that may feel like the safest option. Trust me—it's not. Running from fear is like running around a track. You'll inevitably wind up back in the same place again and again until you truly accept it.

So instead of following fear, I recommend showing up for the assignment with grace. Be willing to show up for the assignment once and for all. And trust that the Universe never gives you what you cannot handle.

Step 3: Honor your feelings.

Showing up for the Universal assignment requires your willingness to feel the pain it triggers so you can heal from the past. Many folks on a spiritual path skip this incredibly important step. It's easy to throw an affirmation on top of your fear or try to will it away. But underneath all our difficult experiences are unfelt anger, resentment, and fear.

The practice of healing long-held suffering begins the moment you acknowledge the suffering is there. Give yourself permission to witness your rage, your anger, and your hidden resentments. In Chapter 2 we revisited the stories that you've been projecting onto your life. Now take some time to honor the feelings that live below those stories. Underneath all your fear-based projections are deep, hidden wounds that you've been ignoring because you're afraid of feeling that old pain. Instead of allowing the pain to be present, you project it onto other people, your circumstances, even your physical body. The fearful part of your mind will do whatever it takes to distract you from feeling this pain—because the moment you start to feel it is the moment you start to heal it. We cling to fear out of habit. We're convinced that it's safer to deny our uncomfortable feelings. But what we repress will persist no matter how good we get at avoiding it. While it may seem terrifying to face our deepest wounds, there is always freedom on the other side.

When you begin to slow down and open up spiritually, you may become even more aware of the ways you've been resisting true healing. You may see how your addictive patterns have masked your feelings or how your high-strung energy made you move so fast that you never slowed down long enough to feel. These behaviors are an unconscious form of resistance.

True healing occurs when you give yourself permission to feel whatever feelings live below the triggers. Rather than ending the relationship, leaving the job, or otherwise avoiding the assignments, show up for them fully and completely by allowing yourself to feel all the pain and rage.

When you notice that you're triggered by your Universal assignment, breathe into the pain. Feeling the pain allows it to pass through you, and strips away its power. Letting yourself feel the pain releases you from fearing it. Rather than acting out or pouring all your energy into avoiding discomfort, you can just feel. And when you do that, you can truly embrace the Universal assignment and heal the pattern for good.

It's important to note that as you go deeper into this work, you may begin to uncover feelings or memories that can be disorienting. Often traumatic memories or sensations can come to the surface when you do deep feeling work. Be mindful of this, and if at any point you feel overwhelmed by these feelings, don't hesitate to seek therapeutic support.

If you feel safe to honor your feelings, then you can begin with this simple meditation. The guided meditation audio can be found here GabbyBernstein .com/Universe. The resources link also includes a list of therapists, coaches, and support groups that can help you if you need to address trauma.

Sit in a safe and comfortable space with no distractions.

Breathe in and identify where the pain, anger, resentment, and fear live in your body. Then place your hands onto this area of your body, bringing energy and attention to it.

Breathe slowly and deeply into this area of your body, allowing yourself to feel the physical and emotional pain that dwells in that place.

Continue to breathe deeply into the pain and discomfort. Be loving and gentle with yourself as you explore the depths of these feelings.

On every exhale release the pain.

As you breathe deeper into the discomfort, you'll begin to feel it dissipate. The tension in your body will release, and you'll start to relax.

Continue this practice as long as it takes to feel a sense of relief.

As soon as you feel the tension subside, breathe in deeply and exhale a sigh of relief. Continue this breath for one minute.

Then take a deep breath into the place in your body where you were feeling pain. Hold your breath for a moment while you gently press your hands onto that place. Envision a ball of golden light pouring into this space in your body. On the exhale, release.

Take one last deep breath in and release.

When you're ready, open your eyes.

This meditation can give you a newfound sense of freedom and will help you face your Universal assignment with ease. Practice it daily, or even multiple times a day, allowing yourself to embrace the pain and discomfort. You may get so great at it that you can simply feel your feelings in stillness for one to two minutes and find great relief from the hidden rage, anger, and pain.

Step 4: Call on compassion.

You'll likely notice a sense of peace set in as you begin to feel your feelings, which unshackles you from fear. The next step is to call on compassion. The pathway to healing old wounds is through honoring yourself for all that you've been through, acknowledging the conditioning that you've experienced, and compassionately loving yourself back to peace. Compassion is the antidote to anger, resentment, and fear. Compassion gives you permission to let go and allow deep healing to begin.

The process of compassion begins with your self-talk. How would you speak to an innocent child if he or she was coming out of a meltdown? Think about the loving words and energy you would offer them. Then apply this same degree of love to yourself.

Take a moment to write down some ways that you could speak to yourself compassionately. For instance, when I notice myself stuck in a Universal lesson, I allow myself to feel the feelings of rage and anger, and then I notice that those feelings come from a sense of not being lovable. The fear comes from a belief that I'm not good enough. Upon realizing these feelings, I compassionately guide myself back to self-love. I say things to myself like, "Gabs, you're back in that old belief system again. These stories are so painful, and I honor you for how you feel.

I understand how tough it must be to go through this. I have so much compassion for where you are in this moment. It's safe to feel these feelings. I love you."

These words can catapult me into a place of calm. This is a practice of self-soothing, self-love, and self-compassion.

UNIVERSAL LESSON: THE PATHWAY TO HEALING OCCURS WHEN YOU LOVE YOURSELF SO MUCH THAT THE DARKNESS FROM THE PAST CAN NO LONGER CO-EXIST WITH YOUR FAITH IN THE LIGHT OF THE PRESENT MOMENT.

Once you've undergone the practice of compassionately loving yourself back to your right mind, you're ready to ask the Universe for help.

Step 5: Place your faith in the Universe.

Step 5 is designed to help you learn to rely on the Universe for support and guidance. Remember, the Universe will never give you anything that you cannot handle. No matter how difficult your universal assignment may seem, you can find comfort in the fact that the Universe is always supporting what is of the highest good. By embracing the Universe as your support system, you're no longer relying solely on your own power to solve your problems.

It's okay if placing faith in the Universe is new to you. Every chapter in this book will help deepen your faith and strengthen your relationship with the Universe. So for today, begin your new faithful relationship with the Universe by asking for help with this beautiful prayer:

"Thank you, Universe, for presenting me with this divine assignment for spiritual growth and healing. I am ready and willing to show up for this assignment with love. I welcome your support. Show me where to go, what to do, and what to say. I trust I'm being guided."

Step 6: Take care of your side of the street.

Once you've accepted your assignment and surrendered it to the Universe for healing, you will immediately feel lighter. You'll feel a sense of release in knowing that you've begun the process of healing your old patterns. The more you surrender, the more faithful you'll feel.

But what about the people who play starring roles in your fear-based story? Like in Lance's case, his girlfriend was left in the dark, unaware of the reasons he was so upset. As soon as he began showing up for his assignment, I suggested that he heal the energy between them. The way he did this was by outing his fear and acknowledging the assignment to his girlfriend. He explained to her that he had an old wound that he was now ready to heal. He shared that her jokes were triggering his wound, and he apologized for the actions that resulted from his fear. By outing his fear they instantly felt closer.

We're often afraid of being vulnerable, but vulnerability is incredibly powerful. It creates genuine connection. When you're ready to clean up your side of the street, don't be afraid to be vulnerable. There is nothing sexier than your authentic truth.

Step 7: Welcome healing.

The final step is to allow the healing to occur naturally. All you need to do is have the willingness to accept the assignment, show up for it, and pray for it to be healed. As you continue on with the lessons in this book, you'll deepen your faith in the Universe and be presented with new opportunities for release. Just step back and let the Universe lead the way. You will be amazed by the miracles that unfold.

The Universe will do for you what you cannot do for yourself. All the greatest healing I've experienced in my life has come from an experience that the Universe placed in front of me and not something that I made happen. That's the beauty of a spiritual path. When you surrender and allow the Universe to do her thing, true healing is presented to you. In every moment the Universe is conspiring to bring you toward right-minded thinking and the energy of love. It's your choice to lean toward love or lean toward fear. This entire book is an exercise in leaning toward love so that eventually it becomes automatic. Begin now by accepting your assignment and following these steps.

The payoff to following this plan is that you will no longer feel powerless over your life's circumstances, and you will stop playing the role of victim. Your spiritual path will give you a sense of power you've never known before: the power that lies in the experience of surrender.

Surrendering may seem scary to you right now. That's normal, and I would fully expect you to feel that way. Just keep it simple and begin by surrendering to the fact that you are willing to show up for your Universal assignment. That's the perfect place to start.

When Lance showed up for his assignment, he was able to be vulnerable and authentic with his girlfriend. When he followed the steps, he released the hold his past fear had on him and healed his false perceptions. And while over time their relationship eventually ended on mutual terms, Lance wasn't disappointed. For he knew in his heart that this woman had come into his life for a reason. She was divinely planted at the exact time when he was ready to show up for his universal assignment. Even though they didn't stay together, the relationship was miraculous. The miracle wasn't a lifelong partnership; the miracle was that Lance showed up for the assignment and shifted his perception of himself and the world.

Great relief is available to you too. By showing up for your assignment, you'll deepen your relationships and strengthen your trust in others. You'll learn that it's safe to be vulnerable. You'll no longer feel the need to hide from your past pain because it will no longer have a hold on you.

UNIVERSAL LESSON: FREEDOM FROM THE PAST IS AVAILABLE TO YOU WHEN YOU SHOW UP FOR THE ASSIGNMENTS IN THE PRESENT.

Facing your fears and showing up for your assignments can be terrifying. The inner voice of fear has likely been extremely loud throughout your life. In many ways you've grown to rely on fear to keep yourself "safe." Your fear has made you feel separate from others and disconnected from love. Therefore, this process may bring up a lot of uncomfortable emotions. Welcome these emotions! Showing up fully and completely is necessary for full healing. Take the plunge and trust in this process.

I can testify that when you show up for your Universal assignments, you will be set free. My greatest experiences of healing, recovery, and spiritual growth are all the result of my willingness to do so. If you're not feeling ready to face your assignment, that's fine. At any point in the book, you can return to this chapter and follow this path. Your readiness is crucial to creating this powerful shift.

Let's recap the steps to healing your universal assignments:

- Recognize the assignment and call it by its name: fear.

- Accept that you cannot avoid the assignment and be willing to show up. Your readiness will clear the path.

- Feel the feelings that live underneath the old pain.

- Call on compassion to clear the path.

- Ask the Universe for help, and rely on a power greater than you.

- Take care of your side of the street, and own your part in the situation.

- Welcome healing and expect miracles.

In Chapter 4 I guide you to the next step of surrendering to the Universe. I help you understand how your images, thoughts, and perceptions affect your energy, and I offer guidance on how to strengthen your energetic presence. Stay open and receptive, and enjoy every step of this beautiful journey we are on together.

chapter 4

YOUR VIBES SPEAK LOUDER THAN YOUR WORDS

The first few chapters of this book introduced the concept that your inner stories and ideas have been creating your reality. Now it's time to dive deeper into the practice of understanding how your projected thoughts and words affect your energy field—and how your energy field affects your life. *A Course in Miracles* says, "There *are* no 'idle' thoughts. *All* thinking produces form at some level." When you think positive and loving thoughts and use empowering words, you feel good. But when you focus your thoughts and words on lack, judgment, and separation, you feel terrible. Your thoughts and words can affect your nervous system, your energy, and, really, your entire life experience.

Begin to pay close attention to how your thoughts and words affect your energy. Your energy is your greatest source of power. When you vibrate a high-vibe, loving energy, you will receive high-vibe, loving energy reflected back to you. Conversely when you put out low-level energy, you'll receive low-level energy and experiences in return. Therefore, your power lies in your ability to change your energy at any time to increase the likelihood of being the recipient of high-vibe, loving energy.

Yogi Bhajan, the yoga master who brought the Kundalini teachings to the West, said, "If your presence doesn't work, neither will your word." Being in alignment with your presence means that you allow the energy of the Universe to move through you naturally. It means that you've set aside all limiting beliefs and smallness and realigned with the thoughts, words, and feelings of love. Simply put, your energy is a free-flowing expression of love.

The promise of aligning with your energy presence is that you'll be more connected. This connection creates deeper relationships, synchronistic support from the Universe, easy access to your source of inspiration, and a sense of safety in the midst of uncertainty.

Throughout my speaking career, I've had many magical experiences of feeling in full alignment with the presence of my power. One talk in particular taught me the miracle of being in the presence of my authentic power. I was giving a lecture in Hamburg, and most people in the audience spoke only German. Eighty percent of them were wearing headphones so they could hear the translator recite my talk in German. This was the first time I'd had an experience with a translator. Before walking onto the stage, I prayed and meditated and I asked the Universe for guidance on how to be of service to this group. Then I surrendered my talk to the care of my inner guide. The moment I hit the stage, I heard my inner guide say, "Don't rely on your words. Rely on your presence." This intuition moved me deeply. I began by speaking very slowly. I allowed myself to be moved by the stories I was telling. And I trusted that as long as I was moved by my message, the audience would be moved too.

Halfway through my talk I looked at the audience with their headphones and I said, "I have a request. I'd love for you to take off your headphones and experience my talk through my energy rather than my words." They all were willing to play along, and they took them off. At that moment I began to feel as though I was in an energetic dance with the audience, communicating through a vibration. I noticed people crying and reaching into their bags for tissues. Even without the translation of the words they were able to feel the vibration of my intentions. I completed my talk, and not one audience member had put their headphones back on.

The next morning I flew to London for another scheduled talk. I was the closing speaker at the end of a full weekend event. The audience had seen dozens of speakers from Saturday morning through Sunday afternoon. By the time I hit the stage, they were exhausted. To make matters worse, I arrived late to a green room packed with people. Rather than excusing myself to meditate in privacy, I stuck around to chat and became distracted by all the other speakers. And suddenly I was shuffled onto the stage to give the closing talk to a tired group that was ready to head home. Because I hadn't properly prepared my energy, coupled with the low energy of the audience, I wound up giving a disappointing presentation. It wasn't that I didn't hit my points or follow my outline—I did. The issue was that I hadn't tuned in to the energy of the Universe to teach with my presence. Remember what Yogi Bhajan said: "If your presence doesn't work, neither will your word."

That day I made a commitment to myself and to my lecture audiences that I would never step on a stage without my connection to my presence.

UNIVERSAL LESSON: WHEN YOU EXPERIENCE SOMEONE'S TRUE PRESENCE, YOU'RE REMINDED OF YOUR OWN.

To ensure I show up for all areas of my life with my presence, I have a beautiful practice of releasing fear and aligning with love. Here's how it works.

Step 1: Get out of the way.

The greatest block to our presence of love is the presence of fear. When our fearful thoughts take over, we get caught up in the littleness and cut off our connection to our power. I often get caught up in thought and let my mind wander into the littleness of fear. I sweat the small stuff big-time. I'll obsess over a flight schedule that's months away, or I'll lock into a fearful story about something that could go wrong with an e-mail broadcast.

So what do I do when I'm caught up in my crazy? I recognize the chaotic thoughts as my resistance to love. I witness the thoughts and remember that they are blocking me from my true connection to the Universe. Then I get out of the way.

Through prayer, I allow the loving energy of the Universe to guide my thoughts from littleness and doubt back to love.

I use this prayer: "I step back and let the Universe lead the way."

This prayer immediately releases me from meaningless mind wandering and brings me back to the presence of my power. I say this prayer all throughout the day to keep me in constant contact with the love of the Universe. Use this prayer whenever fear has you in a headlock.

Step 2: Calibrate your energy by meditating.

I meditate daily to enhance my connection to the Universe and fine-tune my energy. In meditation, we activate synchronistic support and connection to the Universe. Meditation strips away doubt, limitation, and fear to reconnect us with the flow of love. While sitting in the deep stillness of meditation, I notice my energy shift as it reorganizes with the energy of the Universe. Calibrating your energy in this way is like a musician tuning an instrument. Once we're tuned-in and connected, we become aware of the synchronicity and support that are around us.

Once, before I gave a talk in Toronto, I sat in a 15-minute meditation to prepare. In this stillness I felt my limbs tingle and my energy shift. Then I started to receive a vision of myself on the stage in front of the large audience. I saw my small physical frame with massive angel wings extending from my shoulders. These wings were nearly 50 feet in length, and they dominated the entire stage. The image brought me to tears. Shortly after my meditation, I stepped onto the stage, and my wings came with me. The way I felt onstage was the same feeling I connected to in my meditation. I had a magical experience with this audience. I showed up with my presence and helped awaken them to their own. Afterward, during the book signing, a woman came up to me and said, "Gabby, your talk was incredibly moving. I felt as though you had angel wings spreading across the stage." I smiled and said, "I did."

The images we receive in meditation can guide us to remember the magnificence of our true selves. Use your meditation practice to tune in to your presence and bring forth your greatest source of power. You can also listen to the audio meditation at GabbyBernstein .com/Universe.

For several years I've been a student and a teacher of Kundalini meditation. Kundalini meditations are very powerful in that they lock you into the energy of the Universe fast. There is a simple and yet profound meditation called Kirtan Kriya that has the capacity to redirect your focus off fear and doubt so that you can feel deeply connected to love.

Kirtan means "song" in Sanskrit, and kriya is a specific set of movements. A kriyas set is designed to bring the body, mind, and emotions into balance to elevate your presence and enable healing.

Kirtan Kriya combines a mantra and hand gestures (mudras) to uplift you and deeply connect you to the divine energy of the Universe. While practicing Kirtan Kriya, you'll chant the mantra *Sat Nam,* which means truth identified, or truth is your name.

The mudras, or finger positions, are important in this kriya (see illustration below).

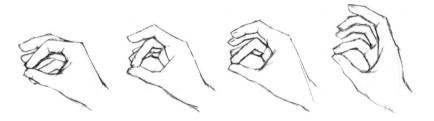

| Saa | Taa | Naa | Maa |

Here's how you practice the Kirtan Kriya:

Sit comfortably in a chair or cross-legged on the floor.

Roll your shoulders back and straighten your neck. Get your body into a straight alignment to become a vessel to receive the love of the Universe.

Repeat the mantra Saa Taa Naa Maa as you tap your thumb on your pointer, middle, ring, and little fingers (as seen in the image on page 58). While you chant the mantra, imagine the sound flowing in through the top of your head and out the middle of your forehead (your third eye point).

For two minutes, sing in your normal voice.

For the next two minutes, sing in a whisper.

For the next four minutes, say the sound silently to yourself.

Then reverse the order, whispering for two minutes, and then out loud for two minutes, for a total of 12 minutes.

To end the meditation, inhale very deeply, stretch your hands above your head, and then bring them down slowly, sweeping out to the side.

Practice this Kriya for 12 minutes (or less). I recommend that you chant along to the music found at GabbyBernstein.com/Universe.

Practicing Kirtan Kriya for 12 minutes a day has been shown to reduce stress levels and increase activity in areas of the brain that support memory. Use this meditation practice to slow down and tune in.

Step 3: Set empowering intentions.

The intention to be in your presence is enough to realign you to love. Setting an intention can be as basic as stating to yourself (silently or out loud) that you're ready to reconnect to your presence. This statement sends a message to the Universe that you're willing to release fear and align your thoughts and energy with love. Whenever you notice yourself out of alignment, set the intention to come back home. Your intentions are far more powerful than you can imagine.

Think about the intentions you set throughout your day. Are you intending to get things done quickly? To achieve and accomplish? To avoid negative outcomes? To just get through the day? What would happen if instead you intended to feel good?

UNIVERSAL LESSON: YOUR INTENTIONS CREATE YOUR REALITY.

A story about my friend Jessica illuminates the power of intention. Jessica complained constantly that she was the only single girl in her group of friends and struggled even to get a date. All her thoughts, words, and energy focused on the problem of not having a partner.

As her friend, I finally got to the point where I had to intervene. I explained to her that all the energy she expended telling herself and the world that it sucked being single and that there were no great guys was *not* helping her get a date. I showed her how her negative focus was lowering her energy, thereby making her really unattractive to prospective dates. I challenged her to set a new intention. Instead of spending her days complaining that there was no one out there, I suggested that she focus on the possibility that there was.

Willing to take my advice, over a three-week period Jessica redirected her focus and began each day with the intention to focus on attracting a partner. She got super into online dating, she spent time in social settings that really lit her up, and she changed the way she talked about dating. Instead of complaining about how bad it was, she started to say things like, "I'm manifesting my partner, and I'm preparing myself for when he comes." She was empowered by her intentions and her words. Within a month she landed two awesome dates, and within four months Jessica was in a serious relationship.

UNIVERSAL LESSON: THE UNIVERSE PICKS UP WHAT YOU PUT OUT.

Does Jessica's story resonate with you? In what ways are you blocking the flow of positive energy toward what you desire?

If you're ready to redirect your focus, you can begin now by setting a new intention. Choose to turn your negative thoughts and energy upside down. Identify the area of your life where you've been blocking the flow of love and set a new intention. Maybe you'll intend to have more fun or to focus on what you do have rather than what you think you lack. Turn your fearful projection upside down, and start extending a new perception that's backed with love.

Set your new intention and write it down now.

Now that you have a clear new intention, say it aloud throughout the day. When you wake up in the morning set your intention with conviction. When you fall back into a fear cycle during the day, set your intention again. As you stay committed to your positive intentions, you'll begin to experience the energy of the Universe supporting you.

UNIVERSAL LESSON: ENERGY FLOWS WHERE
YOUR INTENTION GOES.

Step 4: Understand the power of joy.

Empowering intentions bring us joy, and joy is the catalyst for all that is good in this world. My friend Robert Holden says, "When we commit to joy we increase our chances for success." I love that statement. But many people have chosen, consciously or not, to lean toward fear. In some way, we get lost in the story that pain has purpose, or we buy into the belief that a meaningful life requires struggle. These limiting beliefs can have devastating consequences.

In reality, the more joyful we are, the more light we shine on the world, the more power we have to express our presence, and the more positive energy we put out.

That place of power is the source of the energy necessary to show up and serve, the inspiration behind creative solutions for seemingly hopeless problems, and the access to generosity for giving more where there is need.

Even one person's presence of joy has the capacity to leave a massively positive imprint on a local community and a global landscape. The energy of peace, love, and joy has the power to shift the world. Maharishi Mahesh Yogi was a spiritual teacher who founded the Transcendental Meditation movement in India in the 1950s and then brought the practice to the West. He predicted that if one percent of a population meditated, the coherence of the group would have the power to improve an entire population's quality of life. He believed that the unified field, joy and calming energy, of the group would have the capacity to bring increased peace and harmony to the rest of the community. Maharishi theorized that when groups of people meditate together with shared intentions for peace, their alpha brain waves become synchronized. That coherence of brain waves then causes people who are not meditating to receive the same properties in their subconscious minds.

Maharishi's prophecy was proven right in a study published in 1976. A group of monks was sent into a crime-ridden community. In this case the number of monks sent represented one percent of that community's total population. The monks practiced meditation in the community, and, over time, the crime rate dropped by an astounding 16 percent. This phenomenon—the power of meditative joyful energy to shift the energy of the collective conscious—is called the Maharishi Effect. The reason the Maharishi Effect works is because the meditating group's alpha brain waves are functioning at a powerful level, able to permeate the atmosphere to reach people in the same geographical region to have a positive effect on their hearts, minds, and actions. For more on this topic, see David W. Orme-Johnson's 2003 article "Preventing Crime through the Maharishi Effect," in the *Journal of Offender Rehabilitation*.

When a critical mass of meditators comes together, their practice can bring order to a society and even to the entire planet. Carl Jung, the iconic psychologist and psychiatrist, said:

> Our personal psychology is just a thin skin, a
> ripple on the ocean of collective psychology. The
> powerful factor, the factor that changes our whole
> life, which changes the surface of our known
> world, which makes history, is collective psyche,
> and collective psyche moves according to laws
> entirely different from those of our consciousness.

Deep within our own awareness we have a direct line to the unified field of energy. Through prayer, meditation, positive intentions, and joy, we can enliven that field and create a ripple effect of peace in the world. If you make joy your priority and tune in to this joy daily through your meditation, not only will you feel deeply connected. You will also have a huge impact on the people and circumstances in your life and the lives of people you don't even know. You have the power to be a spiritual activist. Through your positive energy you can bring forth great healing to everyone around you. The energy we put out is either polluting the planet or healing it. Which do you choose?

UNIVERSAL LESSON: WHEN YOU'RE IN A STATE OF JOY, YOU LEAVE A POSITIVE IMPRINT ON EVERY BEING IN THE WORLD.

You have a variety of mindful tools you can now call on. Use the tools from the first three chapters to shift your perceptions, and use this chapter's new practices to cultivate the presence of joy, happiness, and peace in your life. This will strengthen your faith in the Universe and bring forth the power of your presence.

Once you tap into this power, you will start to notice real change. People will want to be around you. They'll feel elevated by your presence, possibly without even knowing why. You'll be more vibrant and energetic, more attractive in all ways, even smarter and sharper— and you'll feel it too. Most important, you'll feel a sense of power in a world that all too often makes us feel utterly powerless. When the tragedies of the world seem overwhelming, you'll now recognize this feeling as a separation from the love of the Universe. By meditating and activating your alpha brain waves, you send loving vibrations to the world, dissipating that separation to co-create joy and peace with the power of Universe behind you.

Step 5: Lean toward joy, and you will be led.

Now that you understand how your thoughts, words, intentions, and energy can influence the world, make a commitment to lean toward joy and peace.

Take a moment to reflect on the following questions. Jot down your answers in the space below or in a notebook.

What brings you joy?

How can you proactively create more joy in your life?

How can you bring joy to the areas of your life that are not joyful?

What would your life be like if joy were your priority?

I spent decades leaning toward fear. But as I progressed on my spiritual path, I began to think, *What would my life be like if I just leaned toward joy?* This question led me to conduct a personal experiment. I started to measure my success based on how much fun I was having. I went on a quest for fun. I began test-driving new hobbies, laughing at my small-minded thinking, and going out of my way to seek joy in all situations—especially the more difficult areas of my life. Whenever I'd notice myself getting stuck in a negative story, I'd challenge myself to try to see it with a joyful perspective. I'd say to myself, "What if I just chose for this to be fun?" Asking myself that question in any given moment immediately catapulted me back into a place of joy.

Seeking joy doesn't have to come only from new hobbies or fun experiences. Joy can come from a decision to have more fun. You don't have to struggle to make your life more joyful! Joy is a choice you make.

Here's an example. Let's say you hate being stuck in traffic (goes for most of us, right?). This is a situation that you're usually powerless over. You need to get to where you're going, and you're slowed down by outside circumstances. In this instance you have two choices. The first is to sit in traffic totally pissed off, silently (or loudly) cursing the cars next to you and honking your horn. This negative attitude makes you frustrated and may even cause a fender bender because you are so angry behind the wheel. Does this scenario sound familiar?

Now let's take a look at option two. You're stuck in traffic, and you take a moment to witness your frustration. Instead of flipping out, you say a prayer: "Universe, thank you for helping me find joy in this situation." In an instant you begin to lean toward joy. Instead of focusing on all the reasons that you hate being stuck in traffic, you choose to seek ways to make it fun. You play that audiobook you never have time to listen to, or you call a friend you haven't spoken to in weeks. Your decision leads you to experience joy in a seemingly joyless situation. Then the time flies by, and before you know it the road is clear.

This lesson may seem obvious, but it can be surprisingly hard to grasp at those times we need it most. Leaning toward joy is not our default. But the more we practice this principle, the more natural it becomes. You have the power to shift the energy of a tormented relationship, change the vibe in your office, or heal your perception of yourself with one choice: the choice to lean toward joy.

When joy becomes your priority, making decisions becomes easier, relationships become more loving, and you start to trust that the Universe has your back. As you choose more loving thoughts, more empowering words, more moments of prayer, and longer stillness on your meditation pillow, you'll begin to experience and express joy naturally. This will give you the freedom you long for. It will open the floodgates for the Universe to support you in ways you couldn't possibly imagine.

Step 6: Celebrate the support from the Universe.

When you're connected to your joyful presence, you attract support from the Universe. For instance, after my talk in Toronto when I felt my angel wings on the stage, I went to the green room to gather my belongings and head to the airport. The only people left in the green room were my friend Julie, her husband, and me. We sat together for a moment to connect, and then I got up to leave. When I stood up, Julie's husband noticed a small charm on the table. He picked it up and said, "I don't know why, Gabby, but I think this is for you." He handed me the charm. It was an angel wing with the word *receive* on it. I said to him, "Yes, I do believe this is for me." I trusted that the charm was a gentle reminder that my commitment to the Universe was being recognized.

I returned to Toronto one year later to give another talk. After the talk a young woman ran up to me and said, "Gabby, I'm so happy you came back to Toronto! I saw you last year. I left you a gift with one of the stage managers. It was an angel wing that said *receive* on it." I gasped. In that moment I embraced the true meaning of living in my presence and accepting support from the Universe. That angel charm was no happy accident; it really had been mine all along.

These types of experiences become the norm when you fully surrender to the presence of the Universe and allow it to move through you. Celebrate the moments when you find yourself in sync with the Universe. This connection is available to you all the time. Bring energy and enthusiasm into the path of reconnecting and it will be a joyful process.

Let's recap the lessons from this chapter:

- Get out of the way of the loving flow of the Universe. Use this prayer to realign yourself with the energy of the Universe and set the process in motion: "I step back and let the Universe lead the way."

- Calibrate your energy through meditation. Your meditation practice recalibrates your energy back to the frequency of love.

- Set the intention to connect to your presence. Energy flows where your intention goes. Each day you can set new and powerful intentions. Be unapologetic about what you desire, and trust that what you focus on will grow.

- Understand the power of joy. Remember that joy is the catalyst for all that is good in the world.

- Lean toward joy, and you will be led. Stay committed to joy no matter what.

- Celebrate the support of the Universe and enjoy the synchronicity, guidance, and gentle reminders that you're on the right path.

Practicing the tools I've offered so far will open you up to a way of perceiving life that is far different from anything you've ever known. You'll soon begin to experience the miraculous flowing love of the Universe by your side.

Once you begin to get in sync with the Universe, some really groovy things happen. In Chapter 5 I share personal stories from my life and from the lives of friends who have had the great privilege of flowing with the guidance of the Universe. These stories will empower you to begin your own co-creation with the energy of the Universe. My hope is that the coming chapters will help you dive deeper into the realm of infinite possibilities for a divinely guided life.

THE UNIVERSE WORKS FAST WHEN YOU'RE HAVING FUN!

In 2014 my husband and I spent nine months hunting for a new apartment. We live in New York City, which is a competitive market that can make renting or buying real estate challenging. In addition, our search happened to coincide with one of the best seller's markets in recent history. Consequently, each new viewing would leave us more and more depressed. Our reaction to everything was, "Ugh, another overpriced, craptastic listing!"

We quickly lost sight of the joy that comes with buying your first home. Instead we started to feel terrible because we were getting priced out of neighborhoods that we didn't even want to live in. The whole experience was bringing us down. In time we started to get sick, fight, and lose faith in our dream home.

Then one night, after spending three hours in Brooklyn touring overpriced apartments all in need of gut renovations, we both unraveled. My husband was angry

and reciting his mantra, "This is un-fun. This is un-fun."
I was getting frustrated because we'd spent so much time
and energy trying to find something that didn't seem to
exist. Then, in the midst of a mini meltdown, I said the
magic words to my husband: "There has to be a better
way. Let's pray for a creative solution. " He nodded yes,
and we prayed. I said, "Thank you, Universe, for opening
us up to creative possibilities. We surrender our plans to
you. Show us what you've got." Within seconds we both
felt lighter. A smile came over me as I settled into the
feeling of surrender. And my husband was now smiling
too. He was thrilled that we'd finally released our need
to control. In our surrender we'd realigned with the true
source of power—the Universe.

In that surrender, an inspired idea came forth. I
said to my husband, "Honey, you know how we always
dreamed of living in the country? Why don't we reverse
our search and check out some houses upstate?" He
looked at me with excitement and said, "That sounds
fun." We were back in action! Forty-five minutes later, my
husband had found four listings in the country. Within
24 hours we'd connected with a real estate agent and set
up a tour of all four houses, including a really awesome
one on a mountain. That Sunday we headed north.

UNIVERSAL LESSON: THE UNIVERSE WORKS FAST WHEN YOU'RE HAVING *FUN*.

The first house we visited was the Mountain House.
As we approached it, my husband said, "This is the one. I
can feel it." We pulled into a magical driveway, hundreds
of yards long, that wound its way up a steep path cut
through the woods. The drive emptied into a charming
world of English gardens and stone walls. Here and there,

marble objects and unusual plantings joyfully played with the beauty of the natural landscaping. Surrounding the front of the house were trees displaying every color of foliage. And the centerpiece of the living room was a view that stretched for miles. Seeing this for the first time was at once exciting and calming. The moment we walked into the house, I felt a rush of loving energy move through my body. I said to my husband and the agent, "This makes no sense, but I feel at home." We went on to look at a few more houses, but none of them seemed to make us feel as good as the Mountain House did.

Over the next few weeks, we visited the Mountain House several more times to get additional information about the property. On our fourth visit, we invited our parents along to get their opinions. The day before our parents' visit, I was on the phone with my dear friend Colette Baron-Reid, who happens to be a powerful psychic medium. I was telling Colette all about the Mountain House. I shared my excitement and my uncertainty. She said, "Have you asked for a sign?" I replied, "A sign, what's that?" She went on to explain that whenever she moves into a new home, she asks for a sign. Her sign is a dragonfly. She said that when she found her last home, she knew it was hers when she saw a book in the house with a dragonfly on the cover.

I loved the idea of asking for a sign. I said to Colette, "I really dig the dragonfly. But my sign will be an owl." I have no idea why I chose the owl. Maybe the owl chose me?

So we set off to visit the house with our parents. The moment we arrived, I noticed a gift card on the kitchen table with a dragonfly on it! I took that as a preliminary sign. Though I'd found Colette's dragonfly, I was still committed to finding my owl. So I scoured the house searching for the owl. I was looking for the owl everywhere—on books, in the trees, even on dishware. By the time we were ready to leave the house, I still hadn't found my owl. I texted Colette and said, "I didn't find my owl, but I found your dragonfly!" She replied, "Great! We were talking about the dragonfly so that's enough. :)"

Colette's reply calmed me down, and we got in the car to head home. Before we got on the highway, my husband and I stopped in town for a coffee. When we were walking back to our car, I turned to the left and glanced at the bumper of a car next to ours. On the bumper was a sticker of a massive flying owl. I screamed, "I found our owl!" It was a big sign that the Universe had our back.

A few weeks later, we made an offer on the house, and it was accepted instantly. As excited as we were, we were also very nervous. Because this was our first home purchase, we were both wary of getting too excited before the paperwork was signed.

In the process of negotiating the final terms on the contract, we traveled to London because I had several speaking engagements. While I was in London, my fear began creeping up on me.

Rather than let fear and uncertainty get the best of me, I chose to pray about it. I had an intimate conversation with the Universe. I said, "Thank you for showing me once again that I am on the right path. Universe, I think I need more owls . . ."

When you're in alignment with the highest good, the Universe works fast. Within an hour of saying this prayer I started to see owls everywhere. There were graffiti street art owls, owl pillows in store windows, owls on clothing. Owls all over London!

Later that night I had a speaking engagement at a beautiful church in London called the Saint James Cathedral. The lovely soundman at the church always gives the speakers a postcard adorned with one of his paintings. In the past he's given me a painting of a bear. This night he showed up with two paintings. He said, "I knew your husband was coming, so I brought you both a piece of my art." He handed the first painting, a bear, to my husband. Then he said, "I'm not sure why, but I had a feeling this one was for you . . ." Then he handed me a painting of an owl! In this moment I sighed with relief knowing that the Universe truly had my back. I thanked him for the gift and thanked the Universe for the sign.

Two weeks later, my husband and I closed on our Mountain House.

The moment we were willing to shift our internal projections, we shifted our perceptions. When we turned to prayer and inner guidance, we were led to creative possibilities.

UNIVERSAL LESSON: LIMITLESS GUIDANCE IS AVAILABLE TO YOU WHEN YOU SURRENDER TO RECEIVE IT.

Logic, fear, and limitation cut off our connection to creative possibilities and universal guidance. Once we surrendered to our true power, miracles began pouring in. And fast. Through the process of remembering and accepting our energetic power, we were able to regain faith and get excited.

The Universe is an abundant flow of positive, powerful energy. When you align with that loving, powerful force of energy, you become a magnet for more of it. When you get psyched about something and lead from a place of joy, immediately the Universe starts to show you the way. You have the power to align with whatever it is you want to see. This alignment will always be positive and supportive to your life as long as you're in tune with your energetic power.

In the case of the apartment hunt, my husband and I had gotten so involved in the stories of the overpriced, "craptastic" real estate market that we'd completely forgotten about our energetic power. In fact, we diminished it with every negative thought, feeling, and comment. The story we built up is what brought us down.

The good news is that we can choose to perceive it differently. By simply opening up to creative possibilities and surrendering, we allowed the Universe to do her thing. Within one short conversation, we were able to come back to our power, release our fear story, and reconnect with inspiration and love.

UNIVERSAL LESSON: RECONNECTING WITH YOUR POWER BEGINS BY REALIZING THAT YOU LOST IT. . . .

Here are the steps we took to reconnect with the Universe. Use these steps to remind yourself of the powerful connection you can tap into at any given time.

Step 1: Be determined to see with love.

What are you saying (out loud or to yourself) that's disconnecting you from your power? For instance, do you often complain to your friends about how difficult it is to find a romantic partner and how hard it is to date at your age? Or do you get home every day only to vent about how much you hate your boss and your job, wishing you could leave but telling yourself the market's too tough to make a move?

Get honest with yourself. Once you've identified your low-vibe story, take a moment to get real with yourself about how it makes you feel. In my husband's and my case, our low-vibe real estate story was literally making us sick. We were so depressed and anxious that we started to fight and argue for no reason.

Take a moment to recognize the way your words and beliefs are blocking the support of the Universe. What is the number one low-vibe story that you have on repeat, and how does it make you feel?

Write it down now.

Getting real about this story is everything. Your honesty is what opens the door for you to remember and accept your hidden power. Take a moment to reread your low-vibe story and how it makes you feel. Then immediately say out loud, "I am determined to see this with love. I surrender this story and let the Universe do her thing."

Make this your mantra. Whenever you notice yourself stuck in your low-vibe story, witness it and say,

I am determined to see this with love.

Be the nonjudgmental witness of your fear and surrender it to the Universe.

Step 2: Let your feelings navigate your path.

The next step in unlocking your hidden power is to get clear about how you want to feel. In my case, I was more focused on finding a home that logically made sense than finding a home that made me feel *at home*. Once we let go of logic and let our feelings navigate us, the Universe stepped in.

UNIVERSAL LESSON: BE UNAPOLOGETIC ABOUT HOW YOU WANT TO FEEL.

In Chapter 4 I led you to begin your commitment to joy. Now it's time to embrace it fully. Take a moment to get crystal clear about how you want to feel. What does it feel like to be in a place of joy?

What do you want to manifest into your life, and how do you want to feel? Write about it now.

Step 3: Ask for your sign.

This is the fun part! It's time to ask for your sign. Remember, asking for a sign means that you're willing to collaborate with the Universe. It means that you're committed to releasing structure and control to instead be led by a power greater than yourself. If you don't get your sign, that's a sign too! Asking for clear guidance is an exercise in receiving good, orderly direction that is unrelated to what you think is right. Remember and trust that the Universe has a better plan than you do.

You can ask for a sign to guide you toward anything you desire. If you're unsure about a decision or you simply want to know you're on the right track, ask for a sign. And don't get hung up about what your sign should be. Just choose the first thing that comes to your mind. Maybe you think of an animal or a song or a book title. Just let whatever comes to your mind become your sign. Let it come to you naturally and commit to what you hear.

Often people receive signs as numbers in sequence like 1111 or 444. Or maybe your sign is a song, a fragrance, or a name.

Without overthinking, decide what your sign will be. Write it down now.

Step 4: Turn it over to the Universe, and be patient.

Now let's turn your desire over to the Universe with a prayer: "Thank you, Universe, for offering me clarity. Show me my sign if I'm moving in the right direction."

Now be patient.

Remember, the moment I surrendered my need to find the owl, I created space for the owl to appear. Try not to control your sign. I've had friends try to manipulate their signs. For instance, one friend chose the number 108 as her sign. If she saw a 54 she'd think that was her sign because 54 times 2 is 108. Let's not overreach. Your sign will be crystal clear if you're going in the right direction. And always remember that if it's not clear, then that too is divine guidance. Colette Baron-Reid says that your sign needs to be like a billboard: so clear that you cannot deny it.

Some signs come quickly, and some take time. If you don't get your sign right away, don't worry. There may be some personal fears you need to clear up, or perhaps faith you need to strengthen, before you can get it. If you're not getting your sign right away, consider that your impatience may be blocking it.

Often when we're impatient it is because we do not trust in the outcome. If you're impatient, maybe it's because you're afraid that something won't happen the exact way you want it to or exactly when you want it to happen. Remember that this need to control the outcome stems from your lack of faith in the Universe. There's also the belief that if something doesn't happen in the time frame that you want that something bad will happen. Worse, this places your happiness and safety in the outcome.

When you place your happiness and safety in the outcome, you lose sight of a plan beyond your own. You cut off communication with the Universe and disconnect from all the infinite possibilities that could occur. The key to releasing this control is to surrender your outside needs and obsessions and remember that nothing can take away your true power: the love and peace within you.

The moment you embrace your peace within and surrender the outcome is the moment that the Universe can truly get to work. A powerful example I hear often involves women trying to conceive. I witness many friends obsess over when they'll get pregnant or why it's taking so long to do so. They track their ovulation, they pee on sticks, and they have passionless sex, worried only about the outcome. When that doesn't work, many turn to IVF for help. Interestingly, I've seen many such women conceive just prior to the actual IVF procedure. Why? The impending procedure allowed them to relax and trust in a plan beyond their own, which allowed nature to do her thing.

Imagine if we lived with a presence of peace regardless of the outcome. The key to living with that peace is to surrender. Then, when you think you've surrendered, surrender some more. Trust in the power of the Universe and relax into an energy of receptivity. Stay committed to your prayer, relax, and let the signs from the Universe be your guide. This may seem difficult when you're deeply attached to an outcome, but you'll come to learn that it's actually much easier to surrender.

The Universe loves and supports us all; we just need to remember to realign with the energy of love so that we can receive it. Let your sign be gentle reminders that you are loved and guided.

UNIVERSAL LESSON: YOU ARE ALWAYS BEING SUPPORTED.

Step 5: Welcome creative possibilities.

Of course, asking for signs is just one way we allow the Universe to support us. We should also be open to creative opportunities. The moment my husband and I shifted from the limitations of our practical ideas and opened up to creative possibilities was the moment the Universe stepped in. When we're willing to design our life from a creative place, the Universe can come out and play.

If you're ready to receive creative possibilities say this prayer: "Thank you, Universe, for transforming limitation and doubt into creative possibilities."

Use this prayer when your logical mind gets the best of you and stay open to receive new and innovative ways to perceive your circumstances. Maybe you'll get a message from a friend. Maybe it'll come from a song or a book. Some sort of clear direction toward creative ideas will be placed on your path. Be willing to let go of what you think you need and allow the power of the Universe to lead you.

Practicing the lessons in this chapter will help you tap into a more playful energy. Your willingness to play, have fun, and be creative opens up your channel to communicate with the loving energy of the Universe. Joy is the ultimate creator. I find that when I'm not having fun, I feel blocked and stuck, and my inner guidance system is shut down. Then the moment I choose to realign with fun and creativity, I feel energy begin to flow and tingle throughout my body. That fun, joyful energy is right in line with the love of the Universe. This is partly why children experience far more wonders and delight than adults do. We must tap into our childlike self and commit to unlearning the limitations of the world to remember the playfulness of our true essence, which is love. In this state you will receive your signs and guidance will become natural.

What would happen if you chose to be more playful and have more fun? This concept may bring up resistance because we're taught to live in the opposite way. We're taught that we must struggle to achieve and that success comes from "making things happen." We learn that good things don't happen without a lot of blood, sweat, and tears. I challenge you to move beyond these beliefs of limitation and suffering. I challenge you to accept that you're here to have fun.

Let's recap the steps from this chapter:

- Witness your low-vibe story and how it makes you feel.

- Honor what you want and how you want to feel.

- Choose your sign that will be the gentle reminder from the Universe that you're on track with the energy and flow of love.

- Turn over your desires to the care of the Universe and be patient. Patience is the key to receiving guidance.

- Become open to receive creative possibilities.

Get psyched about your capacity to connect with the Universe. You have denied your power for far too long. Now is your time to receive love, light, and a sense of deep connection.

If you have doubt about this process, have no fear. In Chapter 6 I teach you that even obstacles offer you guidance. When you tune in to the loving frequency of the Universe, everything in your life becomes a divine opportunity for optimal growth, healing, and freedom. Commit to your new prayers and affirmations and open your heart to continue on this beautiful journey of new perceptions.

As I wrap up this chapter, I'm taking a moment to reflect on where I am and how I let fun lead the way. Fun led me to this very moment. I'm sitting at my desk, looking out at the most epic view from my new office in my Mountain House. I smile knowing that the Universe had a plan for me, and I am grateful that I followed the guidance I received.

chapter 6

OBSTACLES ARE DETOURS IN THE RIGHT DIRECTION

One afternoon I was taking a cab uptown with my husband for a meeting. In the cab we had a petty argument about something meaningless. The argument was ridiculous, but it triggered each of us in such a way that we couldn't let it go. Unfortunately, this pettiness had become the norm. We'd been fighting about silly things for several months, and we couldn't seem to find a way out of the pattern. While I deeply wanted to be "right" in these situations, I also wanted to be happy. So after a few minutes of bickering, my inner wisdom snuck in with guidance. I heard, *Pray for healing and resolution.* I called on the Holy Instant and invited in love. I said to myself, *Thank you for re-organizing this for me and helping me let go of the littleness.* I felt his energy lighten.

Following our meeting, my husband and I headed to the elevator to leave the building. The elevator door opened and I said, "Wait, I have to ask one more question." I ran back to the office, got my question answered, and returned to the elevator. We headed down 17 flights and landed on what we thought was the ground floor.

We waited a moment, but the elevator door didn't open. We quickly realized we were stuck! This was the second time in a year that I'd been stuck in an elevator, so I began freaking out. Remembering that my husband was claustrophobic, my fear multiplied. The first few minutes of being stuck felt like an hour. We were sweating, peeling off layers of clothes, and pacing back and forth while trying to communicate with the building manager through the elevator emergency phone. The building manager kept saying the repairman was on his way. In New York City, though, "on the way" doesn't necessarily mean "soon." For all we knew, the repairman might have to contend with an hour's worth or more of traffic. We were stuck with no clue when we'd get out.

About 10 minutes into the experience, I heard my inner voice again. The voice of wisdom said to me, *Zach is going to freak out. You must be the light!* I got the message loud and clear and redirected my focus onto my husband. I started tickling his back, rubbing his ears, and talking to him about all the things he's interested in. I even let him talk about how *he* wanted to design the kitchen in the Mountain House. I was doing all the things he always wants me to do. I was giving him love, focus, and attention. In this moment stuck in the elevator, my focus was redirected on what truly mattered—my connection to my husband. And it worked! Twenty more minutes went by, and my husband was staying calm. He was enjoying his massage and we'd thought up some creative design ideas for the house. His claustrophobia hadn't gotten the best of him—rather, he was at peace.

Then around the 45-minute mark I began to get antsy. I said a loud prayer: "Universe, we need your help! We're ready to get out of here. . . ." Within minutes we heard the repairman working on the door. Soon after the door opened, and we saw we were stuck between the first and second floors. We gathered our stuff and jumped out of the elevator into a crowded lobby filled with people returning from lunch. We were relieved to be out. My husband looked at his cell phone, and the time was 1:11 P.M. We gasped with delight knowing that the number 1 in sequence is a sign that the Universe is guiding you. Doreen Virtue, the author and medium, says that when you see the number 1 in sequence that there's guidance around you.

With this experience the Universe offered us a beautiful spiritual assignment, a gentle reminder that obstacles are detours in the right direction. Though it may seem like a nightmare to be stuck in an elevator with your claustrophobic husband for 45 minutes, in truth it was a blessing. In the cab I prayed for a miracle to get out of our cycle of ongoing petty arguments and reconnect with my husband. And on that day the Universe locked us in the elevator until we could restore our connection and love.

When you ask for guidance, the Universe may throw you a curveball. Sometimes divine lessons come in odd forms. In our case, being stuck in that elevator got me to let go of all the littleness and restore my thoughts back to love and my energy back toward my husband. When everything was removed, we could realign with what is true, which is love.

This story reminds us that every situation can be seen as a powerful opportunity to allow the Universe to redirect our path. When we call on the Holy Instant through prayer, we realign with the energy of love. Then our loving consciousness expands and we become receptive to guidance that may be far different from our own plan. Our only job is to trust that whatever we've been guided toward is exactly the direction we need. Even situations that appear to be obstacles are actually opportunities—detours in the right direction. Always trust the direction of the Universe and know you're being guided toward love.

UNIVERSAL LESSON: OBSTACLES ARE DETOURS IN THE RIGHT DIRECTION.

A Course in Miracles says, "Miracles rearrange perception and release you from all lack and isolation." Practicing the Holy Instant and entering into a miracle mind-set is the clearest path toward grace. Clear direction may not always be presented to you immediately, but know you're on the right path. This knowing is crucial to your happiness and peace. When you get into the "know" and accept that even the most difficult obstacles can be divine intervention, you can deepen your faith in the Universe.

When you choose to see your obstacles as detours in the right direction, you can begin to find a deeper meaning and personal growth amid the discomfort. Maybe you can connect to a higher purpose, make a real connection to someone, or even be set on a path that will redirect the course of your life in an ultimately positive way not otherwise possible. All obstacles that are perceived with love can be transformed into the greatest life lessons.

Throughout my life I've met many people who have heroically shown up for their detours with a miracle mind-set and as a result shifted the course of their lives and the lives of others. A powerful example is my dear friend Kris Carr. It's likely you're familiar with Kris— she's a well-known leader in the wellness and personal growth world. On Valentine's Day in 2003, at age 31, Kris was diagnosed with a rare form of stage 4 cancer.

Through a tremendous amount of spiritual practice, love, and inner wisdom Kris was able to rise above the fear of the world and embrace the love of the Universe. She was able to see this life obstacle as a divine detour in the right direction. Kris's perceptual shift has led her to become a transformational healing voice for the masses. Kris knows that freedom from fear is the true healing—and the story she is here to share. She loves her body for all that it is, and she embraces her life obstacle as her greatest opportunity to serve and grow spiritually. Kris is my hero.

What would it be like if we all harnessed our own inner Kris Carr? If we were able to face fear with a miracle mind-set and reorganize our fear into purpose and love? How different would our world be if everyone lived in this way?

This is my mission: to guide you to choose love no matter what so that you can turn all obstacles into opportunities for spiritual growth.

The key to trusting in the Universe's plan is to let go of all outcomes. When we get hung up about how something "should" turn out, then we disconnect with the flow of universal guidance. The energy behind a "should" mentality is controlling and manipulating. The Universe does not align with that energy. Therefore, we cut off communication and receptivity. It's when we let go of the outcome that we open up our perceptual worldview and allow ourselves to be led.

My former coaching client Sarah spent many years dating a certain type of man—the guy she thought she "should" be with. On paper these guys had all the credentials: looks, money, compatible religious faith, and shared values. She thought she was on the right path toward creating a long-term relationship, and yet, time and time again, these relationships abruptly ended. Each time her boyfriend would seemingly end things out of nowhere, saying something like, "I'm not sure why I need to end this. You're so great and everything I thought I was looking for, but for some reason I don't think I'm the right guy for you." By the time I met Sarah, she was 40 years old, single, and at her wits' end. She came to me for private coaching to try to "fix" whatever was wrong with her so that she could maintain a relationship.

After four months of coaching Sarah, I could see how she was always looking for a very specific person. She had a narrow set of guidelines and high expectations. Her need to find the "right" kind of man was greatly limiting. She was clearly blocking an awesome opportunity because she wasn't letting the Universe guide her. She was relying on her own strength and needs, trying to fulfill a limiting belief that a "good man" came in just one type of package.

I presented this theory to Sarah, and after a little pushback she began to cry and said, "Gabby, I agree. For my entire life I've been trying to attract the man my mother always wanted me to be with. My father was absent in my life, and my mother taught me that I would be happy only with a successful Catholic man who made a lot of money and could provide for me. So I've been obsessed with finding the man of my mother's dreams."

I honored Sarah for her willingness to see her fearful pattern. I went on to share that her controlling energy was likely the reason she hadn't been able to sustain a long-lasting relationship. Each man could feel her fear and controlling vibe and intuitively knew they were the wrong fit.

It was time for Sarah to reorganize her perceptions and realign with the power of the Universe. The first step was to help Sarah see how she had been blocking her connection to the guidance of the Universe. I needed her to understand how all her perceived obstacles were actually detours in the right direction. Her failed relationships were the Universe telling her that her mother's idea of her ideal man wasn't necessarily her ideal man. I also helped Sarah see how her controlling energy, backed with the fear that her mother had instilled in her, was unattractive, making it almost necessary for any man to want to walk away.

The next step was to help Sarah release her needs and expectations and surrender to a guidance and wisdom beyond her logic and reason. It was time for her to turn to the Universe for help. I offered her a prayer that would help her let go of control and embrace flow. The prayer goes, "Thank you, Universe, for helping me see beyond my limitations. Thank you for expanding my perceptions so that I can attract genuine love."

For more than a month Sarah recited this prayer daily. As the days went on, she began to feel a deep sense of relief and happiness. She loved the idea that she no longer had to figure everything out and that she could finally let go of her need to control her romantic relationships. Sarah's capacity to let this prayer reorganize her energy was the miracle she had been longing for. For the first time, she felt complete without a romantic partner.

Embodying the confidence of knowing the Universe had her back, Sarah became superattractive. Out of nowhere all kinds of men were asking her on dates— men she'd never expected to even find her appealing. These men were far different from her mother's idea of a great man, but they were awesome nonetheless. One man in particular, Michael, was very persistent. Logically, Michael made no sense to her. He was struggling with his career and had no kind of financial security. Also, he wasn't Catholic. In other words, none of the characteristics Sarah thought she had been searching for. Nevertheless, she continued to say yes whenever Michael asked her out.

After a few months of casually dating Michael, Sarah called me out of the blue. She said, "Gabby, I've never been happier in my life. Michael makes me feel so safe, confident, and secure. I love being around him. I feel like he was waiting for me all this time. I'm so glad I opened up to receive him." Ten months later Michael and Sarah were engaged.

Sarah was right: Michael was waiting for her. And the Universe knew. Each man who broke up with Sarah along the way may have seemed like an obstacle, but in reality each was a detour guiding her to shift her energy, rely on the Universe, and trust in a new direction.

UNIVERSAL LESSON: THE UNIVERSE WILL DO FOR YOU WHAT YOU CANNOT DO FOR YOURSELF.

Let Sarah's story inspire you to finally let go of whatever you've been holding on to. In what ways are you blocking your Michael? Whether it's a romantic partner, a career transition, a health choice, or a cross-country move, how are you controlling your experiences and misaligning with the flow of the Universe?

Let me take you through the step-by-step process that helped Sarah see her obstacle as a detour in the right direction and allow the Universe to guide her toward love.

You can apply this practice to any area of your life and you can trust that the Universe will hook you up.

Step 1: Is the word *should* blocking your flow?

In what way is your "should" mentality co-creating the obstacles in your life? Write down the area of your life where you're focusing on the "shoulds" and manipulating the outcome:

Write down your shoulds now.

Step 2: Pray to surrender your shoulds, and see your obstacle with love instead of fear.

The next time you get hung up in a victim mentality over why something isn't working out the way you planned, simply say this prayer and realign with love:

"Thank you, Universe, for helping me see this obstacle as an opportunity. I will step back and let you lead the way."

This prayer will offer you a way through every block. Test-drive it today with something simple. Maybe you feel stressed and overwhelmed by your work life. Say this prayer, and let the Universe reorganize your day. Or maybe you're caught up in a family drama, and you can't release your resentment. Say this prayer, and let love take over. Let this prayer rearrange your perception and move you beyond limitation and doubt.

Step 3: Turn it over.

Turn over your obstacle to the care of the Universe through this beautiful meditation. In this meditation I call on a group of angels to support your practice of surrender. Whether you believe in angels or not doesn't matter. All you need to do is allow the images in this meditation to represent symbols of faith that help you release your need to control.

You can read the guidance below and lead yourself through the visualization, or you can download the audio at GabbyBernstein.com/Universe.

Sit comfortably on the floor or upright in a chair.

Close your eyes.

Roll your shoulders back and lengthen your spine.

Take a deep breath in and hold it. Then on the exhale, release. Take another deep breath in, honoring all that you have been holding on to, and on the exhale release it.

Continue to breathe long and deep throughout the rest of the meditation.

Imagine yourself sitting comfortably in a safe space that you love. See yourself at ease.

Settle into this space and know that you are held, protected, and supported.

Now take a moment to acknowledge the area of your life that you've been controlling. Allow yourself to feel whatever feelings arise when you focus your attention on this situation. Honor what comes up for you, and continue to breathe long and deep.

In your mind's eye, begin to hold a vision of a small golden basket placed in front of you. This basket is illuminated from the inside out.

When you're ready, gently place the area of your life that you've been controlling into the basket. Offer it up, and surrender it fully.

Set the intention now to fully release the need to control and allow the Universe to take over.

Take a deep breath and honor your devotion to surrender.

Now hold a vision of a beautiful angel stepping behind you. The angel gently places their hands on your back and assures you that it is safe to let go of your need to control. Then the angel picks up the basket and flies away with it, waving good-bye.

You have released it to the Universe, and it is being taken care of.

. Sit in stillness for a few minutes as a new relaxed energy settles in.

Then when you're ready, gently open your eyes to the room.

Once you've practiced this meditation, you can trust that the Universe has heard your call. This practice helps you set a powerful intention to release your need to control and embrace a new pathway. Now that you've surrendered your obstacles, it's important to be open to whatever plan the Universe has in store for you. It's very likely that the plan will be far different from what you expected or hoped for. Remember that the guidance you're receiving is leading you in the right direction, even if it feels like a detour at first. Stay committed to that truth, and you'll feel fully supported.

Let's recap your steps:

- Accept that obstacles are detours in the right direction.

- Get honest about how you're controlling certain circumstances in your life.

- Then use your prayer: "Thank you, Universe, for helping me see this obstacle as an opportunity. I will step back and let you lead the way."

- Practice the guidance meditation to lead
  you into a surrendered state of patience
  and peace.

Trusting that your obstacles are detours in the right direction helps you align with the power of the Universe and gain relief. In Chapter 7 I guide you toward the next important step in trusting the Universe: the practice of certainty. Certainty will serve and support you in ways you could never imagine. This next step is crucial to your happiness and peace.

CERTAINTY CLEARS THE PATH FOR WHAT YOU DESIRE

In 2005, early in my sober recovery, I was busy reading all types of self-help books, watching Hay House DVDs, listening to spiritual podcasts, and soaking up all the guidance I could get my hands on. There was one DVD in particular I just loved. The DVD was called *You Can Heal Your Life*, and it featured many of the authors whose faces graced my bookshelves, including Louise Hay, Christiane Northrup, and the amazing Dr. Wayne Dyer. It was Wayne Dyer's part of the film that I found most moving, and I would watch him on repeat. I fell madly in love with his profound one-liners, such as, "As you think, so shall you be" and "You see it when you believe it." These became my mantras, and through Wayne's guidance I began to place great emphasis on choosing the thoughts I desired to co-create my own reality.

Each day I took Wayne's advice and willingly suspended my disbelief. I'd let go of all limitation and allow my mind to dream. I held visions of writing spiritual books in which I would express the incredible healing and growth I was experiencing. I saw myself as a speaker and teacher. I would create images of myself leading talks alongside these great teachers and offer guidance to audiences who, like me, longed for personal growth and healing.

I stayed true to my visions, strengthened my certainty, and trusted that the Universe was supporting my work. My certainty gave me a sense of peace. I never felt the need to push my career ahead and instead trusted there was a plan. The Universe responded well to my peace of mind. In time my certainty turned into form, and my visions became my reality. In 2009 I signed my first book deal for *Add More ~ing to Your Life: A Hip Guide to Happiness*. As soon as I received a galley of the book I sent a copy to Wayne Dyer. I mailed the book to an address in Maui with no expectation of getting a response. Along with the book I enclosed a thank-you note to Wayne for helping me turn my visions into form. It felt amazing just knowing I had sent the book, regardless of whether he got it.

A few weeks later, I received a letter in the mail postmarked from Maui. I opened the envelope to find a handwritten note from Wayne Dyer! He thanked me for the book and encouraged me to continue moving forward with my career. I was blown away by his generosity and love. I couldn't believe he took the time to respond to me.

Several months later I attended a Hay House event in New York City where Wayne was the headline speaker. I was sitting in the front row, hanging on every word. Midway through his talk, Wayne grabbed a book from a table on the stage and started talking about a young new author who had published her first book. He said, "This young woman will be on this stage one day speaking to an audience this large. She will be a fantastic teacher, and I want you all to go out and buy her book." He then said, "Gabrielle Bernstein, please stand up and say hi to the audience." I was shocked—I hadn't realized that he was talking about me! I stood up and waved to the audience and thanked Wayne for his generosity. That moment was better than anything I'd dreamed about.

Three more years passed, and in that time I published another three books. The visions I held of being a speaker, author, and spiritual teacher were coming into form. The more I enjoyed the process and focused on the service and joy behind my work, the more it was supported by the Universe. Then, one day in 2014 in New York City, I walked out onto the stage at the Javits Center to give a talk. Stepping onto the stage and looking out at that big audience, I realized this was the exact stage where Wayne had stood years before, foreshadowing this moment. My longtime vision had come into true form. "As you think, you shall be."

Hard work, passion, and commitment can bring you all the support you need to fulfill your life's purpose. Certainty of outcome, however, is the secret ingredient. When we are certain, we can relax into a sense of knowing and faith. My all-time favorite passage from *A Course in Miracles* is, "Those who are certain of the outcome can afford to wait and wait without anxiety." This passage gives me a sense of power. We all long for certainty in our lives, but our world feels anything but certain. We have grown to believe in fear, powerlessness, and doubt. The messages in this book are meant to challenge these limiting beliefs and encourage you to take on a new perspective—one that lets you learn to trust fully in a path and a power greater than you. When you let yourself dream big dreams, and learn to rely on your inner wisdom, you will receive the gift of certainty.

UNIVERSAL LESSON: THE PATH TO CERTAINTY REQUIRES A PROFOUND DESIRE TO BE FREE FROM FEAR.

My commitment to freedom from fear gave me the strength to embrace certainty in an uncertain world. The freedom I speak of is an inner peace that can come only from genuine faith in the Universe. When we choose to believe in the faith of the world, we are afraid. But when we lean on the faith of the Universe, peace becomes real.

Freedom and peace are frequently under attack, particularly when you feel powerless over a situation. In our lives, many situations arise that seem to be out of our control— the loss of a loved one, a frightening diagnosis, or news of a terrifying world event—and as a result, we lose faith.

Even when everything is seemingly going great, we can lose faith. It's common for me to hear stories of people who, thanks to their committed spiritual practice, have manifested awesome lives. And yet the presence of fear knocks them down. They tell themselves stories like, "This is too good to be true" or "It's too good to last." And just like that, certainty proves them right. But it's okay. Understand that we are programmed to have more faith in fear than certainty in love.

Allowing the creative flow of love to move through us is the feeling we long for. Oftentimes, we look for that feeling in a drink, a romantic partner, or some kind of worldly success. Looking back at my addiction, it's clear I was searching for that creative flow too, just in the wrong place. Once I got sober, I shifted my search inward to realign with the energy of love. My commitment to my inner life through prayer and meditation strengthened my faith and certainty in the love of the Universe. I learned that I could simply step back and allow the creative force of love to work through me. This is when I truly began living.

The following lessons will strengthen your faith on the path toward certainty. The *Course* says, "Trust would settle every problem now!" Practice these lessons and you'll begin to experience a sense of certainty no matter what's going on in your life. Add up the moments of faith to surrender to certainty.

Step 1: Get ready.

Readiness is the first step on the path toward certainty. Are you ready to detach from the narratives, fears, and limitations of the world? Are you ready to put your greatest visions above the littleness of your fear? Are you ready to let go of the past stories, experiences, and circumstances that led you into doubt? If the answer is yes, then you've begun the journey toward certainty. Remember, you don't need to know how you'll let go of these limitations; you just need to be ready.

What would you do if you lived with faith and certainty? Write down your answer.

Releasing doubt will give me the certainty and faith to _____.

Commit to this statement and set certainty in motion.

Step 2: Think it. Feel it. Believe it.

The second step on the path to certainty is to remember that your thoughts and visions create your reality. Much like how my visions of being on the same stage as Wayne ultimately became my reality, you too can create the world you want to see.

To help you in the creation process let's practice a meditation in which I will guide you to align with your greatest desire. In the meditation allow yourself to experience an emotional connection to your desire. Let go of the outcome and enjoy the feelings of desire knowing that the Universe will respond to your positive emotions.

UNIVERSAL LESSON: THE FREQUENCY YOU EMBODY SUPPORTS THE EXPERIENCES THAT YOU HAVE.

Creation Meditation (you can download the audio guidance at GabbyBernstein.com/Universe):

Before we begin, make sure you have a notebook and pen beside you. You will use them immediately following the meditation.

If you like to meditate to music, I often recommend using a certain mantra for this visioning meditation. This Kundalini mantra is: *Ek Ong Kar Sat Gur Prasad Sat Gur Prasad Ek Ong Kar.* This mantra means that there is one creator of all creation. This mantra is the only Kundalini mantra that comes with a warning. Whatever you're thinking about while listening to or singing the mantra will manifest in your life. You will be in such a state of manifestation that your thoughts will have even more power than usual. Simply stay aware of your thoughts while listening to the mantra and consciously choose to lean toward what you desire.

You can download the mantra at GabbyBernstein .com/Universe.

Begin your meditation in silence or with the mantra.

Sit comfortably on the floor or a chair and close your eyes.

Roll your shoulders back and straighten your spine. Place your palms on your thighs facing upward to receive the energy of the Universe.

Take a deep breath in and expand your diaphragm. On the exhale allow your diaphragm to contract. Continue this cycle of long, deep breaths throughout your meditation.

Take a moment to think of a desire that you've carried for some time. Possibly a romantic love that you hope for, a sense of physical or emotional peace, a baby, or even reaching a place of clarity and inspiration.

Honor your desire now.

Now lean into this desire even more.

Begin to imagine yourself living out this intention. See yourself walking hand in hand with your romantic partner. Or see your body free from pain and illness. What images come to mind? Simply allow your mind to wander and bless you with creative visions.

Honor whatever visions come to mind. If at any time during your meditation you feel a sense of doubt or fear, simply honor the feeling.

Feel it in your body and allow it to pass. You don't need to push away the fear or doubt. Just allow it to come and go throughout your creative meditation journey. Honor the feeling, and then return to the vision of what you desire.

Continue to commit even more to the visions you desire.

Breathe even deeper now, and allow your breath to align your physical energy with the emotions of your creative visions. Let the feeling of the vision move through you naturally.

Sit comfortably for 5 to 10 minutes in the energy of this creative flow.

(If you choose to listen to the mantra in your meditation you can chant along with *Ek Ong Kar Sat Gur Prasad Sat Gur Prasad Ek Ong Kar.*)

When you're ready, gently take a deep breath and release them. Then open your eyes to the room.

Immediately following your meditation open a notebook. At the top of the page write: Thank you, inner wisdom, for writing through me. I invite the loving energy of the Universe to take over and lead me to a place of certainty.

Free-write for 10 minutes. Write down the visions you received. Let your pen flow, and don't edit a word.

Step 3: Get into a dialogue with the Universe.

Afterward, take a moment to reread what you wrote. Allow yourself to be moved by the inspired ideas that came through you. Let yourself be vulnerable and connected to your visions. Let the Universe communicate messages or reassurance through your free-writing exercise.

In some cases you may not have written anything connected or inspired. That's fine. New relationships don't always flow at first. Getting into a relationship with the Universe takes time, commitment, and conviction. This is the first exercise in the book in which we actually get into a written dialogue with the inspiration of the Universe. Stay committed to this practice, and bring the free-writing exercise into your daily meditation.

Your practice of welcoming in a conversation with the Universe will be the beginning of a new relationship. When you surrender and allow the energy of love to move through you, many inspired ideas and intuitive thoughts will arise. In time as you continue this practice, more and more loving wisdom will come through. Words and ideas that you never could have come up with on your own will land on the page. Your handwriting might even change, and the lexicon you use may expand. Don't edit your words. Just allow the wisdom to move through you.

The more comfortable you become in this connection, the more certain you'll be that there is a power greater than you working full-time on your behalf. You'll naturally begin to channel the energy of love. In fact, whether we know it or not, we all channel all the time. We're either channeling the thoughts of fear or we're channeling the voice of love. When we pray and meditate, we immediately lock into our connection to love and surrender to higher wisdom. It's our daily commitment to choose love, tune in, and converse with the Universe that sets us up to live with certainty that we're being guided and supported.

Living with certainty is so much fun! You can walk through life with a sense of safety, security, and power. You'll no longer feel disconnected from others and out of alignment. You'll know a new sense of connection that you can't get from any kind of material goods, titles, awards, degrees, and so on. This connection is everlasting and trusting and it sets you free.

Step 4: Co-create with the Universe.

The final step in the pathway to certainty is to co-create with the Universe. Tap into the images and emotions that came through in your meditation and free-writing exercise. Keeping those images and emotions in mind, try to feel what it would actually be like to live in that world. Think your way into the experience of what it's like to be living in your desire.

Single, and in my late 20s, I remember longing for a husband. So many of my friends were moving in with their boyfriends and getting engaged. At that time, my true desire was to manifest the love of my life. Instead of letting fear and doubt discourage me, I brought my desire to the Universe for help.

I declared my readiness. I used my creative visualizations and meditation to help me feel the feelings of romance that I longed for. Then I took those emotions with me. Throughout the day, no matter where I was, I'd conjure up the feelings that I felt on my meditation pillow. The feelings of desire, love, romance, and excitement. I'd walk the streets of New York City as though I had a romantic partner by my side. I'd imagine myself holding hands with my partner, close and loved.

This was a very creative practice. I became a super-attractor. After a week of walking around feeling these feelings, I was being asked on lots of dates, guys started calling me out of the blue, and I noticed men checking me out on the street. I was putting out the superattractive energy of love and romance.

If you walk around feeling defeated, doubtful, and sad, the Universe can't supply you with high-vibe positivity. When you walk through life conjuring up the feelings that you want to feel, the manifestation process begins, and your desires are reflected back to you.

Test-drive this practice once a day for a week, and take note of what happens. Tap into your desired feelings and walk around with those emotions emanating from your energy field. Let these feelings of joy and desire support you in co-creating what you truly want to call into your life.

Walking through life consciously choosing how you want to feel, regardless of what's happening around you, strengthens your faith and certainty. You'll feel certain because even if the actual desire has not yet manifested into form it's manifested into your emotions. I spent nine months in the practice of feeling romantic love around me. In that time I felt certain that my partner was on the way. Even when a date didn't work out, or a guy wouldn't call back, I'd quickly return to my desired feeling and regain my faith. That faith and certainty is what allowed me to remain receptive during that time and ultimately attract a loving partner who today I call my husband.

Over time your visions will easily manifest into your reality and you'll truly know what it means to paint the portrait of your life. You'll see clearly how what you create is a direct reflection of your certainty and faith in the Universe. Most important, when you begin to co-create with the Universe, you serve the world in a truly expansive way because you become an expression of joy.

It's important to be mindful of how you use your connection to the Universe. Far too often I've seen people use their connection for the wrong reasons. I often see folks get caught up in obsessive co-creation. For example, consider my friend Sam. Sam spent an entire year obsessively trying to manifest a new job title at work. His strong focus on getting the new title made him come off as needy, controlling, and energetically annoying. The need to "get to a higher place" actually pissed off his boss, and Sam never got the title that he ultimately deserved. I helped Sam see that his controlling desire was actually blocking the support of the Universe. There was nothing wrong with wanting the title, but consider what might happen if Sam's desire was to truly enjoy his work and be of service to his customers, his co-workers, and the company. When you redirect your focus off what you're going to "get" and onto how you want to feel, the Universe can get involved in the co-creation.

When you co-create with a needy and manipulative energy, you may still manifest the desire of your focus, but it's not likely to last. The relationship may come in or some business deal might materialize, but the benefits to your soul and the lasting happiness you seek won't be satiated. You will have shortchanged yourself of the joy and lasting benefits that come with following the steps outlined above. When you're aligned with genuine feelings that bring you joy, then the Universe will support your desires.

Now having said that, recognize that we all get entangled in that ego-manifesting routine. It's to be expected. I want to call it out now so that you can be mindful of it and gently guide yourself back to truth whenever you get caught in the obsession over the "how" and "when" things will manifest. Instead of obsessing about the outcome, focus on how you want to feel.

The way to get your needy and controlling vibe out of the way is to stop praying for what you think you need and instead pray for the highest good for all. Whenever you pray for the highest good, you get your agenda out of the way. You surrender into the Universe's plan and release your own. Remember that the Universe doesn't respond to manipulation—the Universe responds to love.

Certainty brings forth an energy of peace. That is the goal: to live in this world but believe in a peaceful loving world beyond it. Our faith in a world beyond our physical site is what allows for genuine peace to set in. *A Course in Miracles* says, "You are at peace, and you bring peace with you wherever you go." When we accept that inner peace is a choice we make, then our physical worldview changes. Our true acceptance of that peace sets in when we fully embrace a spiritual relationship of our own understanding.

Now I want to let you into my spiritual worldview in an effort to help you design your own.

I believe in angels, spirit guides, ascended masters, and a community of loving entities who are always guiding us to lean toward love and unlearn the fears of the world. I believe that the Universe is the ever-present energy of love within us and around us. I believe that in any given moment we can align with that powerful presence of love through prayer, contemplation, and stillness. We can measure our peace based on our ability to align with this force field of universal energy. I trust in these spiritual guides just as much as I trust in my husband or my mother. I believe in them deeply, and I know they are working through me to strengthen my faith in the Universe. Most of all I believe that we are here in these bodies at this time to learn great spiritual lessons. As we come to embrace the light and transformation within these lessons, we're guided to spread the light to the rest of the world. I nurture this faith daily with prayer and meditation. This certainty sets me free.

It's taken 36 years and many past lives for me to own these beliefs fully. And today I can say with full conviction that my certainty is the greatest blessing I have ever received.

It is my mission to help guide you to know your own certainty. Maybe your faith lies in religious beliefs, or maybe you connect to the Universe when you go for a long run or spend time with your children. I don't care how you find this connection: all I care about is that you establish a relationship with a higher power of your own understanding. The more energy and intention you bring to your faith, the more fearless and free you will be. Your fearless freedom will light up the world.

When we witness certainty in others, we remember a truth that lies within us. It was Wayne Dyer's certainty and absolute faith in the Universe that drew me to him.

His faith strengthened mine. As I write this chapter, I celebrate Wayne's life as he left his body only a few days ago. My heart is heavy, and millions of people throughout the world are deeply saddened by our collective loss. But deep down I know, with certainty, that Wayne's spirit, enthusiasm, and guidance will never leave us.

As we move on with the guidance and practices in this book, I will continue to encourage you to trust in your own spiritual faith. To help you further along your journey of certainty, I welcome you to take a moment to think about what the energy of the Universe, God, or spirit means to you. There is no right or wrong answer when you're committed to love.

Your faith in the Universe will grow and strengthen daily. For now, honor where you are and trust what you believe in today. One day at a time we can lift the veil and move from darkness to light, from fear to faith, and from disbelief to certainty.

Let's recap the pathway to certainty that we covered in this chapter:

- The first step on the path toward certainty is your readiness. Stay willing to be free on a moment-to-moment basis.

- Tap into the feelings you desire through your meditation.

- Begin a dialogue with the Universe through your writing exercise.

- Consciously co-create your reality by tapping into the feelings you desire and cultivating those feelings in moments throughout your day.

- Stop praying for an outcome and instead, pray for the highest good for all.

- Establish a spiritual relationship of your own understanding. It will change and grow, but for today, honor your own relationship to the Universe.

A Course in Miracles says, "I lose the world from all I thought it was, and choose my own reality instead." When you lean on certainty and faith, you change your mind about the world you see. Your faith has the power to turn trauma into healing, conflict into great growth, and fear into love. Deepen your connection to the Universe one meditation, prayer, and positive desire at a time. Let your faith be your guide as you release the perception of the world you thought you knew and embrace true freedom and peace.

In the coming chapter we build on your faith as you begin to recognize how the Universe talks to you. The practices and stories in Chapter 8 will guide you to deepen your daily dialogue with the Universe so that the presence of love takes on a new role in your life. Get psyched for what's in store. . . .

THE UNIVERSE SPEAKS IN MYSTERIOUS WAYS

In 2008 I went on a spiritual quest with my mother to Brazil to visit the medium John of God. John of God channels spirits to facilitate miraculous healing and spiritual growth. My primary intention for visiting Brazil was simply to accompany my mother on her wild journey—I didn't want her traveling all the way to Brazil alone. But deep down I intuitively knew I was meant to be there too.

The night before we visited John of God, our tour guide suggested that we get clear about the healing and guidance we wanted to receive. I remember sitting in my dimly lit room in the Brazilian posada, writing down my intentions in my journal. At the top of the page I wrote this: *I want to truly know God so that I can be free and teach with authenticity.*

My next intention for my visit with John of God was to receive support for my book, *Add More ~ing to Your Life.* At that time, I didn't even have a publisher. But I was writing the book anyway, because I wanted to bring my spiritual experiences to an audience of new seekers.

I wrote down in my journal: *Thank you, spirit, for guiding me to the right literary partners who can support spreading my message throughout the world.*

The next day I brought my intentions to John of God and received his blessing. Throughout my time in Brazil, I met some incredible people, one of whom was a lovely tour group shaman named Heather Cumming. Heather was also John of God's interpreter. At the time, she was finishing the book *John of God: The Brazilian Healer Who's Touched the Lives of Millions*. Also in my group was Setsuko, a Japanese woman who translated spiritual books. Setsuko was in our tour group to experience John of God and meet with Heather so that she could translate Heather's book into Japanese.

Throughout my two-week experience in Brazil, Setsuko and I had many conversations about the literary world. I told her all about my book and how I was ready to receive a publisher. While she didn't know me at all, she felt a strange certainty that my book would have an impact on the world. The day we left Brazil to head home, Setsuko said to me, "Good luck with your book. I hope to translate it into Japanese someday." I smiled and thanked her for her generosity and support.

Within a few months of visiting John of God, I landed the publishing deal I'd been hoping for. I finished and published my book within four months—an incredibly fast turnaround—and I trusted that the Universe was ready to make it happen.

Six months after my book was published, I was visiting the Omega Center, a spiritual center in Rhinebeck, New York. I was having lunch with an Italian friend of mine who was looking for work as a book translator. He asked, "Do you know anyone in the translation field?" I said, "I know only one woman,

Setsuko, who lives in Japan. I wouldn't even know how to get in touch with her. But I'll look into it."

Fifteen minutes later we headed to the Omega Café for tea. As I walked up the steps to the gift shop, I bumped into a man and a woman walking down the steps. I looked up, and it was Setsuko! I yelped, "I was just talking about you! What on earth are you doing in the United States?" She said, "I cannot believe I'm seeing you here. I just bought your book in the bookstore, and I was so proud of your accomplishment."

Setsuko and I sat down for tea and caught up. Within minutes she said, "I know the Universe has guided me to you so that I can translate your book into Japanese. I'll bring this to my editor and see if we can make it happen." With great gratitude we celebrated the Universal guidance and headed our separate ways. This was a wonderful encounter, plus my Italian friend made an awesome connection and received guidance for working in the field of translation.

Three months later I accepted my first Japanese offer for *Add More ~ing to Your Life*, and Setsuko was the translator. Since that time she's bid on my other books—and who knows, maybe she'll translate this one too!

The synchronicity behind this event serves as another powerful reminder that the Universe guides us wherever we focus our energy and intention. When we surrender our intentions and feel energized by the infinite possibilities, we will be amazed by how fast the Universe responds.

You may have experienced these types of undeniable synchronicities in your own life: Maybe you think about a loved one, and they call just as you pick up the phone to dial them; you say something casually, and an hour later it happens. It's likely these moments come and go—and when they do you're amazed because you can't actually believe it. In some ways it seems too good to be true. You may chalk it up to coincidence, but in truth it's much, much more. These synchronicities are the Universe's way of guiding you to exactly what you need. When you tap into the loving frequency of the Universe, you learn to live beyond the limitations of the world and accept good, orderly direction. You surrender your obsession with logic and embrace intuitive direction. You become aware of the great support within you and around you. My goal in this chapter is to help you fully embrace and surrender to this support from the Universe as I show you how to practice using your intentions and connection for the highest good.

Step 1: Understand that miracles are natural.

When we get in sync with the Universe, we begin to experience many miraculous and mysterious synchronicities. These synchronicities may seem wild and unexplainable at first, but the more faithful you become the more commonly they occur. *A Course in Miracles* teaches us: "Miracles are natural. When they do *not* occur, something has gone wrong." What's natural is our peaceful, loving instinct and our connection to the love of the Universe. What's unnatural is the fear that defends against this connection. Fear, along with guilt, separation, judgment, and attack block us from the miracles that are available to us all the time. When we believe in the love of the Universe and allow it to move through us, we are a clear channel to receive great gifts and guidance. When synchronicity does not occur and we do not feel guided, it's a clear sign that we've fallen back into our fearful patterns.

Our spiritual journey is an experience of remembering that we are love. The more we embody this truth, the more miracles we will experience. We accept that miracles are a natural part of who we are. And when we live in love, we live a miraculous life.

Now, I don't expect you to become enlightened overnight and live in love all the time! But let's aim to bring in more love. When the light shines, the darkness cannot co-exist with it. It's time to ignite your inner light and let it shine brightly so that you can own, honor, and embrace your true connection to the Universe. Continue to pay close attention to when you're blocking miracles, and in that instant choose again.

Step 2: Look for love and expect miracles.

This next step is to spend mindful moments throughout the day looking for love. When you deliberately focus your attention on love and joy, then you open the floodgates to receive miracles. Most of us get caught up focusing on what's going wrong. But what if we spent our days looking at all that's going right? Make a conscious effort to look for love throughout the day.

To ignite this process, begin your day with a prayer: "I focus my attention on the love that is around me, and I expect miracles."

Repeat this prayer and feel the power of these words. Know that your willingness to say these words out loud will set you on the right foot. When you look for love, you proactively collaborate with the Universe to bring you back to a miracle mind-set. Remember, a simple shift in your perception is a miracle. The moment that you forgive your spouse and move on from a stupid argument is a miracle. Or when you ask for a sign from the Universe and you get it, it's a miracle. Miracles can be wild synchronicities or they can be simple shifts. The *Course* says, "There is no order of difficulty among miracles."

It's important to celebrate these miracles by saying thank you to the Universe. Thanking the Universe reinforces your faith and trust that you're in sync with a power greater than yourself. Remember that your relationship with the Universe is an ongoing conversation. The best conversations begin with the words *thank you*.

Step 3: Practice noninterference.

Pay attention to how your day shifts when you commit to love. The *Course* says, "You need not do anything." You don't need to "work miracles" or make anything happen. You merely align with your true love nature and allow your eyes to see what you desire.

The *Course* teaches that miracles are habits and should be involuntary. They should not be under conscious control, because consciously selected miracles can be misguided. With this important message, the *Course* reminds us to turn inward and ask for help whenever we disconnect from our miracle mind-set. Miracles become involuntary when we make turning to love a habit. When we detour into fear, we can call on the Universe to help us restore our thoughts back to love. Whenever we ask for help, the miracle will be presented. We don't need to do anything other than be receptive to the guidance that comes. This relaxed relationship with the Universe gives us the chance to be at peace.

UNIVERSAL LESSON: WHENEVER WE FORGET OUR PEACEFUL NATURE, WE CAN ASK THE UNIVERSE TO REMIND US OF WHAT IS REAL.

I once led a weekend workshop at a retreat center for a large group of people. The group opened up quickly and shared a lot of their fears and stories throughout the weekend. Following the retreat I drove back home with my friend Jenny and chatted about the weekend. Jenny said that while she really enjoyed the weekend, she was feeling a bit down because of all the sad stories and energy she had picked up from others. She also told me that for many months she'd been having trouble sleeping because of her fears about world events and some recent personal experiences. She felt paralyzed by fear. I took in what she said and suggested that she may not be creating clear energy boundaries with people and the world. I reminded her that through prayer she could be guided to a healing of the highest good. I suggested that she relax into the prayer, trusting that whatever she needed would be presented to her. We said a prayer, "I am love and miracles are natural. I welcome healing of the highest good."

Moments after the prayer, I remembered a beautiful energy-clearing meditation by a great spiritual teacher named Doreen Virtue. I frequently use Doreen's meditation to clear out any fear, negative energy, or psychic attacks. I told Jenny about it, and she replied, "That sounds cool. Send me the link when we get home."

Ten minutes later we were listening to a mix on my Spotify account. Then out of nowhere, light instrumental music started playing and Doreen Virtue's voice came through the stereo. It was the energy-clearing meditation! This meditation wasn't on my Spotify playlist, and

I didn't even know that it was saved in my iTunes. We started screaming with excitement. The exact healing that she needed came through faster than she could even imagine. She looked at me and said, "Wow—I didn't have to work hard for that. Miracles *are* natural!" Then she shut her eyes and listened to the meditation. Coming out of the meditation, Jenny felt clear, energized, and released from the negativity and tension she had been holding.

When you pray you get out of the way. Making prayer a daily practice will help you feel the flow of synchronicity and universal support all the time. Your connection to the Universe will be present in all things. You'll think of something and it will appear; you'll set an intention and it will come into form. Practice your faith like a full-time job and try not to interfere with the Universe's plan. Your faith and noninterference will make you feel relaxed. That relaxed state is the portal to receive Universal guidance.

UNIVERSAL LESSON: AS LONG AS YOU REMAIN SURRENDERED AND COMMITTED TO THE HIGHEST GOOD, EVERYTHING YOU NEED WILL BE SHOWN TO YOU.

Step 4: Heighten your faith.

The next step in co-creating with the Universe is to create a faith statement.

This exercise begins with a question:

What would your life be like if you knew you were always being guided?

Take a moment to free-write your responses.

What would you do differently if you knew that the Universe had your back?

Do you have spiritual proof that the Universe is in fact guiding you? Write your story. (If you don't have proof yet, you will by the time you complete this book. Feel free to revisit this lesson later.)

Feel the faithful energy that this story ignites. If you don't have your own spiritual proof, it's fine to lean on someone else's story or on any of the stories in this book. Take a few moments to tap into the feelings of faith that these stories ignite.

How does it feel to be in faith?

What does your faith give you the freedom to do or be?

Now let's create a faith statement. This statement helps you access your commitment to the Universe and the positive co-creation of your life. The goal is to make a faith statement that ignites a feeling of love, connection, and inspiration within you. This statement can be whatever you want it to be.

My faith statement is: *I know that the Universe is an ever-present energy field of love. I know that when I align with the energy of love through thoughts, actions, and beliefs, I am given infinite support and guidance. I know that I can co-create my reality with this loving presence so that I can live in joy and spread light.*

Reading this statement out loud moves me to tears. That's the goal. Write a faith statement that moves you from your core. Use some of what you've already written down in your responses above and write a statement that locks you into a heart-centered state of faith in the Universe.

Write your faith statement, and don't edit a word. Write down whatever comes out. Don't judge what you write, and don't try to make it perfect. Just let it flow. You can always expand upon your faith statement, so don't feel stuck in what you write.

Step 5: Commit to your faith statement.

Now that you have a faith statement it's time to have some fun. For the next 24 hours, commit to living in faith. Begin now by reading your faith statement out loud to yourself, followed by this mantra: *I trust in my connection to the Universe, and I have faith I'm being guided.*

For the next 24 hours, walk through life leaning on your faith in the Universe. When something feels in sync, celebrate it as a moment of alignment. When something goes wrong, recognize it as a detour in the right direction, offering you guidance and support. Choose to see all that occurs as loving guidance. Forgive your negative thoughts and actions and immediately return to your faith statement.

If the thought of relying on your faith intimidates or overwhelms you, remember: this should be fun! It's a radical and awesome experiment in what it's like to live with trust in the Universe and a commitment to love. Just for today let's see how it feels to lean toward faith in love *no matter what.*

At the end of the 24-hour period, take some time to reflect on your experience. In your notebook, take an inventory of the miracle moments and write down an honest intake of when you resisted the support of the Universe. If you enjoyed this exercise, keep it going. Continue to test-drive your faith daily. Have fun with the practice of getting in sync with the Universe. If your spiritual practice feels like work, then it becomes just another thing to cross off your to-do list. The more playful and curious you are on your spiritual path, the more synchronicity you will witness. Co-create your experiences with a sense of joy and an open mind. Savor the journey.

While you complete this exercise, you'll get a glimpse of the freedom that is available to you now. Committing to 24 hours of freedom is easy because you know that the next day you can go back to controlling and worrying. As much as you don't like it, you probably feel safe there. But my hope is that you'll find so much joy in your 24-hour experiment that you'll turn to it more often even if it's for short periods of time. Let this practice become part of your spiritual routine. Give yourself freedom breaks from the chaos you create in your mind and your reality. These breaks can be a reprieve from all that you think you need to make happen and all that you think you need to control. Know that you can take an inner vacation whenever you choose, letting in light to allow your creative energy to come forth and attract you to what you desire.

When you take time off from your chaotic and fearful ways, you begin to create new experiences. The fleeting moments of freedom you experience can be very powerful. They are pinpricks of light in the midst of vast darkness. The more often you allow the light to come in, the safer it feels to be free from the darkness. Fear is a habit—and this practice will guide you to make love a new habit that in time will outweigh the pressure of fear.

Bring this practice into your moment-to-moment experiences. Stay in the flow with love. Each day set positive intentions for yourself. Intend to be more loving to your partner, intend to have a productive workday, intend to eat more mindfully, and so on. When you set positive intentions, you send a clear message to the Universe that you're ready to receive support. Your work is done! All you have to do then is be patient, have fun, and believe in miracles.

Practicing these principles doesn't mean that you won't have problems. Conflicts are also a natural part of life and, when dealt with from a place of love, incredible opportunities for learning and growth. And when you commit to this practice, you will experience problems differently. Instead of freaking out, getting frustrated, or trying to force an outcome, your habitual response will be to lean on the Universe for help. You can ask the Universe to reveal to you the great lessons in each problem and remind you to return to love. The more you practice the habit of leaning on a miracle mind-set, the faster your comeback rate will be. The faster you come back, the happier and more peaceful you will become.

Of course, it's easy to accept that we can co-create the good stuff. But what about the obstacles? What about when you're fired out of the blue, or when an unexpected health condition shows up? How are we co-creating these difficult circumstances in our lives? The bad times, just like the good, are a reflection of what we believe to be true about ourselves and our relationship to the Universe. Oftentimes our difficult circumstances reflect the stress, fear, and separation that we carry. It's important to witness the difficult situations in your life through the lens of love. Choose to see them as an opportunity to surrender to your spiritual practice even more. The amount of flow and synchronicity we experience can be measured by the depth of our spiritual connection.

The guidance you desire in any area of life may come quickly or it may take time. And, really, the timeline doesn't matter. In fact, time is irrelevant when you're working miracles. Just stay in the flow and believe. When I reunited with Setsuko and secured the Japanese deal, there was a part of me that wasn't even surprised. My trust in love and my commitment to miracles gave me the strong faith that this manifestation was in perfect alignment with the highest good. The Japanese deal came at the perfect time for the book and for Setsuko. The Universe had a plan for us, and we cleared the path to receive it.

Stay committed to love and get out of the way. That's the gig, folks! It really is that simple.

This empowered way of living is available to you right now. Journeying through life co-creating your reality with the Universe is immensely fulfilling. Living in collaboration with the Universe can change your entire life.

Let's continue your journey of heightening your faith so that you can begin to fully embrace your relationship with the Universe.

Here's your recap of the steps:

- Miracles are natural. Let the Universe support you.
- Look for love in all the right places by repeating this prayer throughout the day: "I focus my attention on the love that is around me and I expect miracles."
- Practice noninterference. Miracles are habits and should be involuntary.
- Create your faith statement.
- Commit to your faith statement and recite it throughout the day.

Your faith will be your greatest resource as we move into Chapter 9. In the coming pages, I invite you to begin the process of undoing fear and fully surrendering to the grace and love of the Universe. Some of what I ask may seem challenging, but lean on your faith statement and we will clear the path to freedom and peace.

chapter 9

ONENESS SETS YOU FREE

Six months into the process of writing this book, I found myself feeling like a fraud. Every so often I'd catch something nasty sneaking its way into my conversations, my thoughts, and my interactions. Even though I was practicing the principles in the book, I felt out of alignment with my true love nature because of one lingering bad habit: the habit of judgment. This judgment was a projection of a disowned part of my own shadow. It didn't matter how often I prayed, how service oriented I'd become, or how long I meditated. My judgmental nature was blocking my connection to the Universe. This behavior appeared innocent enough at first, but it left me feeling sad and disconnected. Judgment quietly but swiftly drained my happiness, reinforced a sense of separation from others, and blocked my connection to the Universe. My neck hurt all the time, and I found myself getting into tense, petty arguments with my loved ones.

I decided I needed to take a close look at what I was thinking, saying, and doing. I lovingly witnessed my behavior and came to realize that judgment was the cause of this disconnect. Seemingly innocent and minor moments of judgment were blocking me from my greatest resources—my presence, power, and capacity to experience the flow of love.

When I began to pay attention to how judgment made me feel, I noticed that each time I judged I came away with low energy and a sense of physical and mental weakness. *A Course in Miracles* says, "The ego cannot survive without judgment. The ego seeks to divide and separate. Spirit seeks to unify and heal." So, if judgment makes us feel separate and compassion and understanding make us feel whole and unified, why do we spend so much time in judgment? It's partly because of the world in which we live. So much pop culture and media place a tremendous value on status, looks, and material wealth. We are made to feel "less than" without this or that possession. We use judgment to avoid the feeling of our own inadequacy, insecurities, and lack of self-worth. It can feel easier to make fun of someone for a perceived weakness than to look at our own sense of lack. Judgment and separation form the basis for so many of today's problems. Without judgment we would see one another as equal. We'd have no feelings of better than or less than. We'd be one. Oneness is our true nature. When we're in tune with the feeling of oneness, then judgment and separation dissolve and our connection to the love of the Universe is restored.

After witnessing how judgment weakened my power, I decided to change my ways. I put myself on a path of clearing judgment so that I could release the pattern of separation and strengthen my experience of oneness. While tough at first, in time my judgmental nature began to subside. In fact, I no longer resonated with it. Very soon after, I found myself surprised by new business opportunities, interesting connections that I had longed to make, and stronger and more intimate personal relationships. Even my neck pain began to subside. Freeing myself from judgment instantly cleared the space for more love.

In some ways releasing judgment can feel like letting go of a friend you know (deep down) is not good for you. Even though in your heart you know it's time to move on, you feel a sense of sadness, loss, and disorientation. It can be scary to fully let go of judgment because it is a pattern that we grow to rely on. We use judgment to avoid the feeling of our own inadequacy, insecurities, and lack of self-worth. Instead of addressing those feelings, we look at the perceived shortcomings of others so we don't have to face our own pain. However, projecting our judgment onto others only serves as a temporary reprieve. Not only do our own feelings of inadequacy not dissolve. To make matters worse, we also feel an unconscious sense of guilt for judging others.

Whenever you become aware that you're not feeling at peace and your life isn't flowing naturally, that's a clue that you've decided to align with the wrong mind of judgment.

Judgment shows up in many ways. For instance, any time you think another person is your source of happiness or pain, you're in judgment. Often judgment shows up as jealousy, comparison, and envy. Judgment can be sneaky, presenting itself as justification for condemning someone you believe has wronged you. However, this judgment is what keeps us in the illusion that we are separate from one another.

I experienced this lesson firsthand at a dinner party. My husband and I went to a friend's home for a get-together. When we arrived we were escorted into a small room with six people eating appetizers and having drinks. There was a woman in the group who seemed to be dominating the conversation. She was speaking loudly, boasting about her career, and making sure that the conversation revolved around her. This behavior really triggered me. I kept thinking, *Who does she think she is? Why is she speaking so loudly? How can I get a word in?*

To combat her bombastic behavior, I started to speak loudly too. I made sure everyone knew who I was and how much I had going on. I went out of my way to be seen and heard. I was so annoyed by this woman, and I became determined to make sure I could get my voice heard.

Soon after we sat down to dinner. Thankfully the annoying woman was seated at the opposite end of the table, so I wouldn't have to listen to her ridiculous stories. Although she was far away, I noticed her staring at me throughout the meal. This made me even angrier. *Why was she staring at me?*

After dinner everyone stepped outside to have more drinks. Because I've been sober for nearly 10 years, I stayed inside. At that moment the annoying woman walked over to me. *Ugh*, I thought. She walked up to me and said, "I noticed that you don't drink." I replied, "No, I've been sober for nearly a decade." She responded, "Me too. I've been sober for seven years."

In that moment all separation dissolved. I recognized myself in her. I was able to see my judgment of her as a mere reaction to a disowned part of my own shadow. Her need to be seen was my need to be seen. Her attention-grabbing behavior was mine too. We were both recovering alcoholics looking for approval and at the same time healthy, sober women proud of our recovery. Her darkness and her light were a reflection of my own. When I was able to recognize myself in her, all boundaries dissolved into oneness.

This experience was a great universal lesson in releasing judgment. What you judge in others is a reflection of what you judge in yourself, whereas what you love in others is a reflection of your light. As Yogi Bhajan said, "Recognize the other person is you."

This experience was a huge universal lesson in releasing separation. My hope is that I no longer have to go this far to remember oneness. I hope I can become more mindful of my judgmental behavior and set myself free.

To truly reap the benefits of this practice, you must be open to releasing judgment in every area of your life. You can't let go of judgment except for your boss, or your mother-in-law, or yourself. You must surrender it all. In some areas of your life, it will feel easy to let it go. In others you'll hold on tightly. Don't worry: this is natural! Freedom from judgment can offer you so much of what you desire. Physical pain can subside, you'll experience emotional and spiritual healing, and a deep connection to the Universe will be restored. *A Course in Miracles* says, "You have no idea of the great release and peace you will feel when you totally give up judgment." Therefore, releasing judgment is crucial if you want to be happy and free.

My four-step process will show you the way. When you commit to following the process and become willing to let go of judgment, all of it will begin to dissolve.

UNIVERSAL LESSON: YOU MUST BE WILLING TO SHED OLD PATTERNS AND EMBRACE A NEW WAY OF BEING.

The lessons in the earlier chapters have prepared you for these steps. You've begun to clear the space to perceive your life with more love and deepen your connection to the Universe. Releasing judgment will guide you even closer to that connection.

Take a moment to access the place within that led you to pick up this book. You were guided here through your conscious or unconscious desire to feel free, to feel happy, and to reconnect with your true nature. Let that fierce desire support this process so that you can fully commit to the steps ahead. Follow this process and clear the tension, negativity, and stresses that are blocking positive flow in your life.

Step 1: Witness your judgment without judgment.

By this point in the book, you are aware that the way you feel either blocks or attracts love into your life. When I started to witness how my judgmental nature made me feel, I could easily identify why my life wasn't flowing. Judgment made me feel weak, sad, and disconnected. It even caused me physical pain. The moment I was able to step away from the judgment and witness how it made me feel, I was able to truly understand how much it was blocking my connection to the Universe.

A friend was distraught because she could no longer feel her connection to the Universe or hear her intuition. In response to her concern, I asked her to rate her daily level of judgment on a scale of 0 to 10 (10 being the highest). She thought honestly for a moment and said, "You know, Gab, I never realized this before, but my judgment levels are at a 9. It feels really terrible to be disconnected from others and myself." Her honest inventory helped her see that it was judgment that was keeping her held back and stuck. Witnessing her judgment was the first step toward changing the pattern.

In most cases we don't even realize how judgmental we are. The way out of judgment begins when you witness the judgment *without more judgment*. Be mindful that when you take an honest inventory of your judgment, you may be tempted to criticize yourself for it, or to feel shame for your thoughts or behavior. Instead take a moment to honor yourself for having the willingness to look with love at whatever choices you've made.

So let's do an inventory of how judgmental you are. Take a moment to rate your daily level of judgment from 0 to 10 (10 being the highest). Get honest with yourself about how judgmental you really are. The best way to measure the level of your judgment is to check into how it makes you feel. The more uncomfortable you feel when you think a judgmental thought, the higher the rating.

Rate your judgment level now.

Next write down how your judgmental nature makes you feel.

Review your notes. Do you see how judgment blocks your loving decisions? Can you feel how it holds you in a place of negativity and makes you believe that you are separate from others? Taking a closer look at the way judgment brings you down will strengthen your desire to rise up.

In contrast, love accepts. Whenever you notice yourself caught up in judgment or attack, remember that you chose to see it from a sense of separation and fear. Once you've accepted that you have made that choice, the only important thing is to choose again. Ask yourself, "Do I look through the eyes of love or the eyes of judgment?"

Accept that you chose the teacher of fear over the teacher of love. Be mindful not to judge your fear with more fear. Don't get upset with yourself for making this choice. Instead, celebrate the fact that you recognized the misguided choice you made and that you're on the pathway to freedom.

Step 2: Forgive the thought.

Let yourself off the hook for the judgment that you made. The *Course* says, "Every communication is either an extension of love or a call for love." When you attack with judgment, you're really just looking for love. The search for love is your true intent behind the attack because deep down all you want is to protect yourself from not feeling loved. It's also the intent of the person you believe has attacked *you*. Both of you are simply looking for love. At its core, attack is a call for help. The *Course* says, "Love always answers, being unable to deny a call for help, or not to hear the cries of pain that rise to it from every part of this strange world you made but do not want."

I want to reiterate this point: Attack, pain, fear, judgment, and any form of separation are merely calls for help. When you're in physical pain, you *know* that your pain calls for relief. The same goes for judgment. It's a form of emotional pain that you want to relieve. Whether you realize it or not, you do not want to remain sick, sad, and fearful. You want to be free. Witness your judgment without judgment, accept that you have chosen fear, and be open to receive the help you're calling for.

This brings us to forgiveness. In any given moment that you witness yourself in judgment, you can become free by simply forgiving the thought. Forgive yourself for having the thought and even forgive the thought altogether.

Recognize that the thought did not come from your highest self. Honor your judgmental self, and remember that you're merely looking for love. Then, as quickly as possible, choose to forgive the thought. You don't need to hold on to the thought. You don't need to replay it.

You can forgive it in an instant. This simple desire seamlessly leads you into the Holy Instant.

Welcome in the Holy Instant with a prayer:

"I recognize that I have chosen wrongly, I forgive this thought, and I choose again. I choose love."

The presence of fear is your resistance to love. The way back to love is through surrendering to the Holy Instant. The instant that you choose love over fear, you rise above illusion and separation and realign instead with oneness. Simply saying this prayer may offer you immediate relief.

Step 3: See for the first time.

We judge others and ourselves through the lens of our past by projecting old experiences onto our current circumstances. This is no different than judging the world through the lens of fear. If, for instance, you had an authority issue with your mother growing up, you may project that same issue today onto your boss by resenting her authority.

We begin to heal our judgment toward others when we accept that people are our teachers in the classroom that is our life. Making that commitment allows us to look differently on our situations. Witness how we drag the past in the current moment, and then choose again. We can choose to look at a person (or situation) as if we are seeing it for the first time. Imagine how free you would be if you didn't bring your past with you into your relationships (or into each encounter).

Practice saying this prayer before every encounter that triggers the shadows from your past:

"I want to see this person for the first time."

When you practice seeing someone for the first time, you release them from the false projections you've placed on them and the beliefs that separate you. Instead of seeing others through the lens of the past, see them as someone calling out for love. Remember that you're both caught in the same cycle of fear and you're both desperately seeking a way out. That way is through love.

When spiritual teachers talk of mankind being "one," the oneness to which they refer is our one desire to be happy and free. We all share that same desire and the same fear. If more of us began to choose love, then oneness would be restored. It starts with you. You have a major part in the healing of the world. The more oneness you create in your life, the more light you shine on everyone around you. I believe this is our biggest mission here on earth. To choose love, restore oneness, and shine our light. This brings us to the final step—a meditation for oneness.

Step 4: Meditation for oneness.

To close out the judgment clearing process, follow this beautiful Kundalini meditation. This meditation is designed to remind us that we all have a shared essence that is beyond our physical site. Practice this meditation and reconnect to the essence to experience oneness in this moment.

Posture/Mudra: Sit comfortably cross-legged on the floor with a straight spine. Place your right fist at your side with the index finger pointing up, and place the left hand over the heart center. You can also do this meditation sitting back-to-back with a partner.

Focus: Focus the eyes at the brow point.

Mantra: I recommend that you play the song "I Am Thine" by Jai-Jagdeesh. You can access the music at GabbyBernstein.com/Universe. The mantra is: *Humee Hum, Tumee Tum, Wahe Guru; I am Thine, in Mine, Myself, Wahe Guru.*

This meditation celebrates the connection we have to others through our shared connection to the Universe. Humee Hum tunes us in to our own consciousness. Tumee Tum accepts that we are one with the other person's consciousness. Wahe Guru means that we are both connected to the Universe. Then we chant, "I am thine, in mine" to project our consciousness of our personal self to the infinite self. Then the world confirms that we are one with the Universe. Finally we celebrate this universal connection with Wahe Guru.

Chant with the music for 11 minutes (or less).

If you're new to chanting mantras, give it a try. I fell in love with Kundalini yoga and meditation because of the mantras. I lose myself in the mantra, and I remember my interconnectedness with the Universe.

I chose this specific Kundalini meditation to conclude the judgment-clearing process so that you can have an intimate experience of what it truly feels like to release the walls of separation and realign with the oneness in your relationships.

Practice these four steps, and stick around for the miracles. Freedom is available to you instantly. It will continue to unfold as you stay committed to releasing judgment. Remember that judgment is a nasty habit. The more you practice these principles, the weaker the habit will be and the more freedom you will experience.

I recently had a wonderful experience putting my four-step process into practice. I was at an 11-day spiritual retreat in San Diego. When the course was complete, I felt awesome and superconnected to the Universe. But then I arrived at the airport to return home and saw that my flight was delayed three hours. It didn't even faze me because I was still in a high-vibe zone from all the meditating and spiritual lessons I'd practiced that week. I sat down to read and relax while I patiently waited out my delay. An hour later it was announced that the flight had been delayed 12 hours. My noon flight now would be leaving at midnight, which meant I'd have to take a red-eye back to New York. Even though I hate red-eye flights (and airports in general), I maintained my calm and surrendered to the change in plans. I had eight more hours to spend in the airport, and I did my best to relax and get some work done.

An hour later I went to the desk to ask about my flight. The attendant replied with a negative attitude and brushed me off as if I was wasting her time. Immediately this sent me into ego separation, aka diva mode. I jumped into judgment and began thinking thoughts like, *How dare you treat me like this?* Separation, judgment, and attack set in. To avoid making a scene, I walked away to grab dinner.

An hour later I returned to the gate to get the update on the flight. By this point I'd been in the airport for more than seven hours and I had several more hours to go. I was doing my best to maintain my Zen attitude, and I peacefully walked up to the desk to ask the attendant for guidance. There were two new flight attendants standing at the desk, but as I walked up the rude attendant from earlier stepped in. She looked at me with an attitude of disgust and said, "What do you want now?" This sent me into a tizzy. I looked at her and said, "You know I've been here for seven hours, and my flight has been delayed for twelve. You know I'm exhausted, and I am desperate to get home. The least you can do is be polite." She went on to assert her authority and tell me that I had been asking too many questions and I needed to calm down. At this point I got a serious attitude and replied, "I'm one of this airline's best customers! I would hope you could be kinder given my twelve-hour delay!" She wasn't interested in my response or my nasty tone. At that point I stormed off.

Raising my voice and fighting back did not feel good. The moment I walked away from the desk I burst into tears. I felt defeated, exhausted, and sad. I sat down for a moment and tapped into my body. I asked myself why I felt so sad. Was it because I didn't get my way? Because I was disrespected? No. I felt this way because I'd succumbed to the ego's sense of separation. I let judgment take the lead. This moment of recognition and my willingness to see my part in the situation was the first step in clearing the aftermath of my judgment outbreak.

The second step was my acknowledgment of how this judgment made me feel—disappointed, physically ill, and saddened.

I was ready to move into the third step of letting go of the shadows of the past. In that moment I decided to see the airline attendant as if I were meeting her for the first time. I chose to see her with no separation. Rather than perceiving her as separate, I chose to see her as one with me. Once again I heard the words of Yogi Bhajan ringing in my ear, "Recognize the other person is you . . . recognize the other person is you."

For further guidance, I called on the Holy Instant for support. I said my prayer: "I recognize that I have chosen wrongly, I forgive this thought, and I choose again. I choose love."

Instantly I felt better. (I guess that's why they call it "the Holy Instant.") I sat in the meditation, listened to my mantra, and allowed the presence of love to settle back in. A glowing sense of peace passed over me. I no longer felt resentment and instead felt a deep connection. I heard the voice of my inner wisdom say, *She is you. Her pain is yours. Her suffering is yours. And you both want the same thing: to return to peace.*

I came out of my meditation, and the judgment had lifted. I could see her as me, and I was free. At this point I calmly read my book and relaxed. A little while later, when I walked past the front desk where she sat, I felt a presence behind my shoulder slow me down. Without thought or planning, I stood in front of the desk, looked her in the eye, and said, "I apologize for speaking to you that way. It was inappropriate, and I hope you can forgive me." She smiled with joy and replied, "I'm sorry you're having such a hard day, and please let me know how I can make it better." This was a miracle moment. I left the airport that night exhausted, hungry, and a little closer to God.

This practice of releasing judgment dissolves all boundaries with love. It brings us back to the truth: that we're all in it together. We all suffer. We all feel unworthy and abandoned. Calling on the Holy Instant allows us to remember that we are all the same, and so we should be kind to one another. Identifying this sameness is what allows us to shift our focus from separation to love. The same way we share the thought system of fear, we also share the loving mind. Most important, we share the same capacity to choose love over fear. As my dear teacher Kenneth Wapnick said, "We see that we all have the same interest of awakening from the dream of unkindness and returning to the kindness who created us kind."

Let's recap the four steps:

- Be willing to release judgment and accept that you have chosen fear.

- Forgive the judgmental thought with this prayer: "I recognize that I have chosen fear, and I choose again. I choose love."

- Let go of the shadow of the past by seeing someone for the first time with the eyes of love.

- Practice the Kundalini meditation, and recognize the other person is you.

This four-step process can set you free one moment at a time. Each time we release judgment and return to love, we experience a miracle. When we add up these miracle moments, we get more deeply aligned with our true nature and the support of the Universe. Whenever you practice clearing judgment, a loving answer and solution will come through for you. As the *Course* says, "All the angels in heaven will come to your aid." Let love guide everything you say and do.

In Chapter 10 I guide you to see how your conscious connection to love can clear the path for peace and harmony.

YOU ARE THE UNIVERSE

I once spent a week in a training course with my friend and teacher Deepak Chopra. The first day of the training, Deepak told us to pair up with a partner and then ask each other a series of questions. My partner was a young woman named Elsa. During the exercise, one partner was asked to whisper a question again and again in the other person's ear, and their partner was meant to respond with whatever thoughts jumped into their mind. We began the exercise with the question, "Who are you?" Slowly Elsa began to whisper in my ear, "Who are you?" And my first response was, "I am Gabrielle Bernstein." She went on, "Who are you?" I replied, "I'm Gabby." She repeated this question a few more times, and I continued to respond with answers that described me, my personality, and who I perceived myself to be in the world.

Then Elsa moved on to the next question: "What do you want?" I replied, "I want a snack." She continued, "What do you want?" I replied, "I want a nap."

This ridiculous Q&A went on. . . .

"What do you want?"

"I want a full night's sleep."

"What do you want?"

"I want a coffee."

"What do you want?"

"Did I say I want a nap?"

After several rounds of questioning, we ended the exercise and went back to our seats. I remember feeling terrible afterward. I thought, *I'm at a spiritual retreat and all I can think about is when I can get a snack.*

I didn't have much time to lament my poor performance during the exercise because Deepak immediately led us into a group meditation. He guided us to repeat a mantra and release any attachments we had to the previous exercises. Within a few minutes, I began to feel relief. Then I slipped into a silent place of stillness in between thoughts. The space where nothing matters. The space where I feel free. I relaxed into the stillness and let go of all the pretenses I'd built up around myself. In that moment I was one with the Universe. Suddenly a loud inner voice spoke up and said, "I am one with the Universe, and I want to get closer to consciousness." I had realigned with the energy of the Universe long enough to remember my true nature. I came out of my meditation remembering that *I am one with the Universe, and I want to get closer to that truth.* This involuntary response instantly brought me to tears. In the presence of truth, all fear disappeared, all separation released, and all judgment dissolved. In that instant I was free.

Later that week, during my training with Deepak, I had the opportunity to sit down with him for a private conversation. I told him about all the spiritual quests I'd been on, all the paths I had chosen, and all that I believed to be true. I said, "Is it okay that I've followed *A Course in Miracles*, Kundalini yoga, John of God, and many other spiritual thought systems? Is it okay that I haven't committed to one specific path?" He replied, "Of course it's okay. You do whatever it takes to get closer to consciousness."

Deepak was right. Our work is to do whatever it takes to get closer to consciousness, and each of us does it in our own unique way. Every exercise in this book has been a gentle guide, bringing you closer to consciousness to remind you of who you truly are. You are the loving energy of the Universe. This truth can blindside us when we least expect it, in fleeting moments on our meditation pillow or in the instant that we choose to release judgment and forgive. Wouldn't it be nice to feel that connection more often?

Our connection to love is often just a whisper amid the noisy chaos in our mind. Fear and separation are a pattern that must be interrupted on a moment-to-moment basis. When we fully commit to shift the pattern through prayer and meditation, we begin to rely on love more than fear. Love becomes our default, and we can redirect our thoughts and energy quickly to return to our truth. This book has offered you a pathway toward releasing the falseness of the world and remembering the truth, which is love. Don't judge your path. Don't try to be perfect. Just focus on your commitment to tuning in to the frequency of the Universe.

UNIVERSAL LESSON: YOU ARE ONE WITH THE UNIVERSE.

The way to knowing your truth is to allow the voice of love to echo through every single thought you have. Even when you detour into fear, *which you will do all day long*, commit to the voice of love the moment you witness that you've chosen wrongly. Don't tolerate the fearful wanderings of your mind any longer. Make love your priority.

Think about how different your life would be if you were fully committed to love throughout the day. Imagine waking up in the morning and instead of turning on the news, overcaffeinating, and checking your phone, you began the day with a devotion, a prayer, or a meditative moment. My teacher Marianne Williamson says, "When we give time to a quieting experience, we have a different life because we have a different nervous system." Tuning in to the love of the Universe lowers our stress levels, restores our cells, and reorganizes our energy. Conscious contact with love interrupts the pattern of fear and returns us to our true nature.

Although this book may seem as if it contains many lessons and exercises, there's really only one: choose love. Each practice brings you closer to it. Each prayer, meditation, and exercise helps shift your focus away from perceiving yourself as separate from the love of the Universe. The *Course* teaches, "Fear can never enter in a mind that has attached itself to love." Each time you shift your focus back to love, you release your sense of separation and realign.

When you're in alignment with the love of the Universe, peace cannot be disrupted. No person, situation, or circumstance can take away your peace of mind. This isn't an easy concept to grasp, because we believe so deeply in fear and separation. We believe we can be harmed, and we protect ourselves at all costs. At the level of the mind, we can never be harmed because in any moment we can choose love. The more we stay committed to love, the more we will believe in it. I can say this with conviction. I have committed my life to unlearning fear and releasing my separate perceptions of myself.

Each new day offers me great spiritual assignments that, when faced with prayer and devotion, bring me closer to consciousness. Even in this moment as I write these words I'm reinforcing that connection.

We are all connected in that we have the same problem and the same solution. Our problem is that we detoured into fear and believed we are separate and unsafe in this world. While we may all have this problem, we also have the same solution. The solution lies in the decision-making part of our mind that chooses love.

It doesn't matter where you are on your spiritual journey—whether you're a longtime Spirit Junkie or a first-time reader—you can accept this truth now: you are one with the love of the Universe. Our spiritual path leads us toward spiritual sight. This is when we begin to relinquish our faith in our perceptions of the world to see strength rather than weakness, oneness rather than separation, and love rather than fear.

At the beginning of this book, the voice of love was probably distant and hard to hear. But the more you lean toward love, the more you begin to see with spiritual sight, listen with the voice of love, and live more joyously and free. This is what it means to release your perception of separateness and accept you are one with the Universe.

Stringing together those moments of true connection is how we begin to see the world through the lens of love rather than the lens of fear. Even when situations baffle us, we have the power to quickly return to love. Now is the time to crank up the volume on your truth and turn down the volume on the voice of fear and separation. So choose it. Fully surrender to your spiritual nature, your purpose, passion, and a deep connection to the Universe.

By this point in your practice, you're ready to embrace your true connection. These steps are designed to deepen your faith that you are one with the love of the Universe.

Step 1: A prayer for truth.

Prayer is the pathway to love. This prayer acts as an intermediary between your feelings of separation and your truth. Use the prayer as an invisible guide back to love. Let each word sink into your psyche. Recite this prayer out loud to yourself.

A Prayer for Truth

"I call on the energy of the Universe to guide my thoughts back to love. I surrender the false perceptions I have placed upon myself. I forgive these thoughts and I know that I am love. I am peace. I am compassion. I am the Universe."

Following the prayer, settle back into the energy of love through the following meditation.

Step 2: A meditation to connect you to the Universe.

You can open your heart to love through this beautiful Kundalini meditation. This meditation will foster a deep emotional and physical connection to the Universe. Kundalini is the yoga of awareness. I am a student and teacher of Kundalini yoga because the meditations and practices instantly bring me closer to consciousness. This Kundalini meditation will move stagnant energy and get you directly aligned with the Universe. The posture in the meditation opens your heart to reconnect you to your true nature and oneness with the Universe.

I recommend practicing this meditation with the song "Halleluiah" found at GabbyBernstein.com/Universe.

Old Gypsy Way of Calling
on the Spirit of Mother Earth

Originally taught by Yogi Bhajan on July 4, 1994

This meditation is meant to help you invoke the loving spirit of the Universe.

Posture: Sit comfortably cross-legged on the floor with a straight spine and a straight neck.

Mudra (hand position): Raise the arms up 60 degrees from horizontal, elbows and wrists straight. Stretch the body forward slightly from the plane of the body. The angle of the palms follows the angle of the arms. The fingers are straight and together, thumbs relaxed.

As seen in the image here.

Visualization: Stay still and imagine a flame at the heart center.

Breath: Breathe consciously, long and deep.

Time: Sit in this meditation for three minutes.

To End: Inhale deeply. Hold your breath for 15 seconds. Exhale. Inhale deeply. Feel in your connection to the Universe. Hold for 15 seconds. Exhale. Inhale deep. Feel the taste of the sweetness of life. Hold for 15 seconds. Exhale.

Following this meditation, lie on your back and rest for several minutes. This is called Savasana. I believe that Savasana is the most important pose because it's where we can really relax into the energy of love. Take your time to lie on your back with your palms facing upward, and allow the presence of light and love to pour through you. It's possible that you may feel a tingling sensation in your palms given the activation of your hands in the meditation. Let the loving flow of energy pass over your body and relax into Savasana. In these moments of genuine release you can reorganize your nervous system and realign your connection to love.

Step 3: Truth is your name.

After several minutes of rest, slowly bring your awareness back to your body. Roll your wrists and ankles in circles and gently come to a seated position. In this seated position, continue to feel your connection to the Universe. When you're seated, take a deep breath in and say out loud *Sat Nam*. Closing a practice with this Kundalini mantra identifies your truth. *Sat* means "truth" and *Nam* means "name." The mantra is translated as "Truth is my name." It is simply an acknowledgment that the magnificence of the Universe is the truth of who you are.

Following this practice you may feel a deeper sense of interconnectedness. If even for a fleeting moment you felt free, then you're one moment closer to consciousness. Yogi Bhajan said, "In the flow of deep meditation . . . my nectar thoughts are filled with

God." Practice this meditation often, and in time your connection to the Universe will become more present in your life. You may even want to practice it for 40 days straight. This meditation has the power to offer you a direct line back to your true spiritual nature. It can remind you that you are the light of the Universe.

In any given moment, you can remember your truth by returning to your mantra *Sat Nam* or the translation, "Truth is my name." To remain happy and free, we must be in communion with our truthful connection as often as possible. This gentle reminder will bring you back home. Practice repeating the mantra *Sat Nam* whenever you're out of alignment with the Universe.

The vibration of the mantra *Sat Nam* manifests truth into your physical experience. The vibration of *Sat* reaches up to the ether, calling on your connection to the Universe. *Nam* is a grounding vibration that acknowledges that you can bring the energy of the Universe into your day-to-day experience of the world. Bring forth your truth in every corner of your life. Bring peace with you wherever you go.

Step 4: Walk the path of humility.

To truly flourish on your spiritual path, you must embody humility. Knowing that you are one with the Universe means that you accept that you're not more special than or separate from others. This may be one of the most challenging spiritual assignments, as we've grown to believe in the stories of who we think we are.

Humility doesn't come easily. At least it didn't for me. While I spent many years deeply committed to my spiritual path, I was equally committed to the outward pretenses I'd built up around myself. Deep down I knew that this ego perception was blocking my connection to love, but it wasn't an easy habit to kick. Thankfully the Universe presented me with a divine assignment that forced me to seek humility, shed my ego, and get right-size.

Here is how it happened. Not long ago, I was left out of an event organized by a prominent teacher in my field that featured a few of my contemporaries. The fact that I wasn't asked to participate seriously bruised my ego. And while I wouldn't admit it to anyone, I was really upset by what I considered a missed opportunity. I asked my publicist to look into it and find out why I was left off the roster. After a little digging, she called me and said, "Gab, this is really strange. When I asked them why they didn't consider you, the women in charge of the event looked at each other silently for a second and then responded that they felt you were self-entitled." I responded with a defensive tone: "Why would they think that? I never did anything wrong." She replied, "They said it was the vibe they got from you."

I sat with this issue for several hours and allowed myself to move through the emotions of frustration and anger. I was defensive, embarrassed, and confused. I couldn't understand what I'd done to make them think that.

After processing my feelings, I chose to seek a spiritual solution. I asked the Universe to show me my assignment. Through deep contemplation and an honest inventory of my behavior, I looked closely at my part in the situation. Even though I thought I'd done nothing "wrong," I remembered that our vibes speak louder than our words. I got really honest about the ways that I perceived myself as special and separate. I got honest about my lack of humility. I came to realize how this extremely uncomfortable situation was the perfect assignment to bring me to my knees and surrender to humility once and for all. Humbly surrendering was the only way I was going to see the shadow that needed to be brought to the light.

I called on a message from my great *A Course in Miracles* teacher Kenneth Wapnick: "We should be grateful for all situations that make us the most uncomfortable, because without them we would not know there is something unhealed in us."

I allowed the discomfort to lead me back to my truth. This universal assignment helped me commit to the path of humility. I could no longer try to dance between spiritual humility and my worldly ego. It was time to surrender it all and accept my purpose: to be love and spread love. Without humility I would never know what it truly meant to be one with the Universe.

Now I devote each day to humbly surrendering to the care of the Universe. In my morning prayers, I turn over my perceptions of myself, I release my needs and expectations, and I allow the Universe to take over. This daily devotion keeps me connected to who I really am.

Walking the path of humility doesn't mean that you give up on greatness. In fact, it means that you embrace your true magnitude and power—the power that lies in your devoted connection to love.

Truly accepting your love nature requires you to relinquish all the stories and pretenses you've created about yourself. It's challenging, but trust that even a brief moment of connection is enough. Many folks who begin to open up to metaphysical truths get scared about giving up the ideas of the world and connecting to love. That feeling is not your truth; it's the voice of fear trying to stay alive. Your faith in fear will make you resist your connection to love in order to keep you in the perception that you're separate from the love of the Universe. It's terrifying to let go of the beliefs you've held on to for your lifetime. But your happiness and peace depend on releasing those ideas. This brings us back to where we began, with our resistance to love. Remember that fear will resist love, especially when love becomes more present in your life. Simply be aware of your fearful resistance and commit to walking the humble path.

Your human experience is part of your spiritual journey, so you don't have to walk through life expecting to live in divine connection all the time. Aim to string together many moments of consciousness to ultimately remember that you are the spirit of love having a human experience.

Let's invite in a moment of consciousness now and give yourself permission to accept your magnitude. As a gentle reminder of how limitless you are, read this passage from *A Course in Miracles*:

> To use the power God has given you as he
> would have used it is natural. It is not arrogant
> to be as he created you, but it is arrogant to
> lay aside the power he gave and choose a little
> senseless wish instead of what he wills. The gift
> of God to you is limitless. There is no circum-
> stance it cannot answer and no problem which
> is not resolved within its gracious light.

Each day do your best to stay in communication with the Universe. Spend your time leaning toward the potential positive outcomes rather than all that you expect can go wrong, turn to prayer when you're in doubt, and meditate to deepen your connection. Whenever you find yourself caught up in conflict, choose to seek creative solutions. Your devotion to your practice will keep you in constant contact with the support of the Universe. Your level of happiness and peace will be a direct reflection of your spiritual practice.

Devoting your days to your inner life will bring you joy. Even though you may still deeply identify as a separate person having a unique experience, you can hold a small place in your consciousness for the truth. That belief is enough to keep you on the path.

Let's recap the lessons from this chapter:

- Do whatever it takes to get closer to consciousness.

- Experience your interconnectedness. Practice the prayer for truth and the Kundalini meditation to heighten your experiential connection with the Universe.

- Remember that truth is your name. Practice the mantra *Sat Nam* to stay committed to your true nature.

- Walk a path of humility to stay centered in your universal truth.

Remember the words of Deepak Chopra, "Do whatever it takes to get closer to consciousness." Stay consistent with your conscious contact to the Universe, and you will be set free. In Chapter 11 you'll deepen that connection through the practice of surrender.

WHEN YOU THINK YOU'VE SURRENDERED, SURRENDER MORE

Right around the time that I began writing this book, my husband and I also began trying to conceive. I had it all perfectly planned. My expectation was to get pregnant right away and then cut back on traveling so that I could relax at home while spending time working on the book and enjoying my pregnancy.

I was very committed to this plan; I canceled speaking engagements, said no to big opportunities, and otherwise took things off my plate to free up my time to take care of myself. My goals were set, and the plan was airtight. But there was one problem: I didn't get pregnant. Month after month I'd rearrange my goals and expectations to try to stay on course with my pregnancy plans. I'd tell all my friends that we were "consciously conceiving," but it was really more like unconsciously controlling.

While I felt strongly that I was meant to be a mother and I intuitively knew that there was a soul ready to become our child, I still couldn't release the plan. I became obsessed with the timing. Otherwise how would I fit pregnancy and a child into my busy life? This future tripping got the best of me. Each month when I realized I wasn't pregnant, I'd go back to zero, break out my calendar, look nine months ahead, and stress about the timing, which I tried desperately to control so that this major life experience wouldn't be inconvenient. My need to control the plan totally cut off my communication with the Universe. I silently judged myself for not getting pregnant, and I compared myself with everyone around me who was conceiving. Worst of all, I'd walk around telling everyone how much faith I had that I'd be a mother when deep down I was suppressing an unspeakable fear that it would never happen.

About nine months into the process of trying to conceive, I went to a New Year's Eve party with friends from college. All the couples there had children except for my husband and me. I felt like an outsider, left out of this phase of life. I sat through dinner comparing myself with everyone at the table and feeling totally defeated.

I woke up the next morning, New Year's Day, and got my period. Here I was again, another month gone by, countless plans reorganized, and still no baby. I spent the first half of the day deeply depressed. I felt caught in a shameful silence with no outlet. My friend Jordan was staying at my house, and somehow I found the courage to tell him how I was feeling. Within moments of sharing my feelings with him, he gently guided me to witness the ways that I'd let fear and the need to control block me from love. He reminded me that instead of comparing myself with my friends with children that I should celebrate them. In the celebration of their love, I would recognize it as my own. Our conversation helped me see how my fixed, rigid agenda had made me lose hope.

After talking to Jordan, I turned to the love of the Universe for healing. I prayed and asked for help in releasing my own plan and accepting a plan far greater. In the stillness following my prayer, I heard my inner voice say, "Your plans are in the way of God's plan." I could see clearly how I had been blocking the higher plan. I accepted this message as a new Universal assignment and embraced the spiritual growth that was presented to me.

As humans, we love to set goals and make plans. It's a smart way to keep our minds organized and not let small daily snags throw us off-kilter. But when we fixate too much on achieving our goals and sticking to our plans, we get in our own way. We become convinced that *we* know what's best. We relentlessly pursue the path of our ego, that loud and misguided voice. And we do it at the expense of cutting off communication with the Universe.

This behavior keeps us from manifesting what is of the highest good for all. In order to allow the presence of love to shine on every area of our lives, we must remember that hope never rests. Hope is the energy that carries us when we lose sight of our spiritual faith. Hope reminds us of the power of love and clears the path toward the highest good for all.

UNIVERSAL LESSON: GOALS OVERSHADOW GUIDANCE

The part of me that wants to be in control doesn't like the word *hope*. To my fearful mind, hope implies that there's something I'm unable to make happen on my own. While I may not like that concept, it's exactly what I needed. Hope helps us move through our problems and choose to perceive them in a new way. Hope is the conduit for miracles. For me to move past the sadness, shame, and need to control, I had to surrender to hope and let go of my plans.

In this process, I was reminded of the need to turn inward for answers. Carl Jung said: "Who looks outside, dreams; who looks inside, awakes." When we look outside for our faith, we get lost in the dreams of who we think we should be, what we think we need, and when we think we need it. But when we turn inward, we surrender to the one and only truth, which is love. When we surrender to love, we can experience our darkest moment as the greatest catalyst for transformation.

The pathway back to hope is through surrender. It's not something that comes naturally to us—it must be a daily practice. Consider my situation. Here I was in the midst of writing a book on how to trust in the love of the Universe, all the while trying to control my own life's circumstances! The need to control is sneaky. It can blindside us. The ego thinks it knows the way, and it does everything it can to keep us in a headlock. The best way, and ultimately the *only* way, to stay connected to the flow you've established is to surrender and then surrender some more.

This is not to say that surrender is easy. I see people struggle with it all the time, especially around money. The fear of turning over your earning capacity to the care of the Universe is terrifying for some of us. We worry that if we're not fully in control of our earnings that we won't be able to pay the bills and life will spiral into chaos. But that controlling attitude blocks others from wanting to hire us, promote us, or buy our products. Surrendering our money to the Universe doesn't mean that we don't go to work and take action. What it means is that we take action from a faithful state: we surrender our financial needs to the love of the Universe while simultaneously showing up for work with faith and grace. Faith and grace, not controlling energy, clear the path for abundance.

Another point of contention is relationships, romantic and otherwise. I witness people trying to control their partners' behaviors or manipulate a relationship. This doesn't necessarily mean they're conniving or uncaring—not at all. They just desperately want the relationship to "look" the way they've decided it should. Controlling your relationships blocks love and deprives you of your spiritual lessons. But surrendering your relationships to the care of the Universe invites love back in. When you let go and allow the Universe to guide your relationships, it's like booking a session with an invisible therapist. The presence of love sets in to the relationship naturally, guidance comes in many forms, and your behavior changes. When you surrender your relationships to love, you're able to bring your highest self to the table.

How about goals and scheduling? If you're anything like me, you really like to have a plan and stick to it. However, overplanning blocks the natural order and puts a limit on what would otherwise be limitless possibilities. When you overplan, you limit your capacity to co-create with the Universe. Rigidly sticking to a plan forces you to rely on your will, which cuts you off from the support and wisdom of the Universe. In my case, my plan was blocking the sacred joy of making a baby. Releasing the timing and schedule was the only way for me to let love lead and clear space for my life to unfold with grace. I had to surrender my plans and expectations to the care of the Universe and trust that love would lead the way.

Surrendering to love is not always easy, but it's absolutely necessary if you want to live a miraculous life. You don't have to surrender fully overnight. In fact, it usually doesn't happen all at once. Surrender is a process. *A Course in Miracles* says, "Each small step will clear a little of the darkness away."

Here are the steps I used to clear away the darkness of control and surrender to the love of the Universe:

Step 1: Take your hands off the steering wheel.

In his book *The Seat of the Soul*, Gary Zukav writes, "Take your hands off the steering wheel. Be able to say to the Universe, 'Thy will be done,' and to know it within your intentions. Spend time in this thought. Consider what it means to say, 'Thy will be done,' and allow your life to go into the hands of the Universe completely."

To restore your connection to the guidance of the Universe, you have to loosen your grip. When you surrender your plans and release control, you stop pursuing the path of your misguided ego. You allow the voice of your intuition and the energy of love to be your guide.

The way to take your hands off the wheel is through prayer. If you're in need of surrender, begin each day with these words:

Today I surrender my goals and plans to the care of the Universe. I offer up my agenda and accept spiritual guidance. I trust that there is a plan far greater than mine. I know that where there once was lack and limitation there are spiritual solutions and creative ideas. I step back and let love lead the way. Thy will be done.

These words will help you humbly surrender to the guidance of the Universe. Something miraculous happens when you let go and allow. You open up to an infinite field of possibilities. The moment I surrendered my desire to be a mother, I felt taken care of. I knew that the Universe was guiding me in the perfect direction, time, and order. Trusting the path of the Universe gave me freedom and happiness in the midst of uncertainty.

Step 2: Turn over time.

The biggest block to living with faith is time. There are many situations in our lives that we cannot control. You can't decide the exact day you'll conceive, the moment that your lover will propose, or a million other things. But you *can* control how you experience each moment of each day. The way to surrender your need to control time is to embrace the present moment. In any moment you can receive a miracle with the decision to choose love. That simple choice, to choose love over fear, can release you of time and restore your hope and faith. Love is a decision, and all that is asked of you is the willingness to choose it. Each time you do is a miracle. And with total willingness your obsession with time will end. The miracle is now.

A Course in Miracles lesson 173 is: "The light has come." I once had a deep conversation with my friend and mentor Robert Holden. We both have a shared love for this lesson. For Robert it's a gentle reminder that the light isn't coming when you get the job or the baby is born. The light *has* come. It's already here. In any given moment, you can surrender to the light and live in the miracle.

To give up our obsession with time, we must accept that the light has come. We already embody all the love, joy, and peace we long for. In any moment, when you find yourself caught up in time, you can return to the miracle of the moment. Accept that the light has come, and live in the miracle. Imagine how free you would feel if you lived your life moment to moment rather than milestone to milestone.

When you turn over time, you can trust in the order of the Universe. You have faith that everything is happening to you in the perfect time so that you can grow and heal. Embrace the miracle available in every moment, and each step will be perfectly laid out before you. Don't rush your spiritual evolution; enjoy it. It's the journey that matters, not the destination.

Step 3: Surrender your goals and let faith take the lead.

We must learn to give up goals and embrace hope and faith. Goals often imply that you need to achieve something else to be happy. Remember, there's nothing wrong with visions, dreams, and desires *as long as you're willing to surrender them.* The key is to gently hold great visions and then release them to the Universe.

To feel free and surrendered, we must learn to release our attachments. Deepak Chopra says, "When you're happy for some reason you're still in misery because that reason can be taken from you tomorrow." Instead of seeking some reason or outcome to make us happy, we must learn to trust in the wonders of the Universe. Each day brings new miracles to celebrate. Each moment can be a miracle if we choose to perceive it that way.

Instead of focusing on goals and outcomes, redirect your focus onto celebrating what you already have. Take time each day to devote your attention to what is thriving in your life. In my case, I gave up the goal of getting pregnant on a specific date and chose instead to focus on the deep love I have for my husband. I made it my intention to feel connected and in love. I redirected my energy onto my body and the health I am blessed to enjoy. I concentrated on my home and the space I am creating for the baby I am ready to call into my life. Instead of focusing on when I will have something (or someone) new, I focused on what I already have.

When you return your focus to what you already embody and enjoy in your life, you can let go of what you think you need. That doesn't mean that you cut off your desire. In fact, it's quite the opposite. You bring far more love and energy to your desire when you take the pressure off. Focusing on what you *do* have creates more of what you want.

Step 4: Turn it over to the holy triangle.

A beautiful element of my spiritual practice is my holy triangle. It's a wooden triangle that hangs above my altar. Each edge of the triangle has a meaning: faith, love, and charity. The triangle is a symbol used in the John of God community to facilitate spiritual surrender. The idea is that when you write down your desire and place it in the holy triangle, the desire will be taken care of. You leave your desire in the triangle for a week, and then at the end of the week you remove the piece of paper and burn it. The act of burning the paper symbolizes your faith and trust that your desire is being supported. (I burn my paper over the kitchen sink. If you don't want to burn it, you can flush it down the toilet.)

When I was wrapping up this chapter, I realized that I hadn't placed my desire to be a mother into the holy triangle. All this time I'd been so controlling that I'd forgotten this crucial step. Placing my desire into the triangle allowed me to tell the Universe that I know it's being handled.

You too can have a holy triangle. You can make one, or if that isn't you, simply use a box. I've taught many people to create their own God box, and it offers the same service as the triangle. You can decorate the box in any way that empowers you. Once you have the triangle or box, try it out. Write down your desire and place it in the hands of the Universe. At the end of one week, take it out and burn it. (Be sure to burn it safely in the sink.) That's all it takes. As you continue on with this practice, be mindful not to put the same desire back in the box. That would imply that you didn't trust it was being taken care of.

This is a powerful practice of surrendering. Practice the three steps above and then offer up your desire to the holy triangle (or box). Place your desire in your triangle, and say a silent prayer to surrender it to the Universe. Turn it over once and for all, and know your request is being heard.

These four steps will greatly help you surrender what you think you need and embrace what is of the highest good for all. Focus on the subtle, moment-to-moment shifts. As *A Course in Miracles* reminds us, "Each small step will clear a little of the darkness away."

You may be wondering how you'll know when you've truly surrendered. You know you've surrendered when you trust that the Universe has a better plan than you do. You've surrendered when you no longer manipulate and force outcomes. You've surrendered when you let go of the need to be in charge of your life and let the Universe get to work instead. Finally, you know you've surrendered when you don't defend your need to control.

Follow this path, and surrender your goals. Here's the recap of the steps to surrender:

- Take your hands off the wheel through prayer.

- Turn over time by accepting the present moment as a miracle.

- Surrender your goals and let faith take the lead.

- Release your desire to your God box or holy triangle. Trust it is being taken care of.

These steps will clear even more space for the Universe to serve as your guide. Once again I'm reminded of the wisdom of *A Course in Miracles*: "There is a way of living that is not here though it seems to be. You do not change appearance but you smile more frequently. Your forehead is soft and your eyes are serene."

Surrender offers you this kind of serenity. When you practice surrender, you'll begin to lean on a power greater than you. In time you'll know it's always there, and you'll rely on it.

chapter 12

BE AN
INSTRUMENT
FOR LOVE

One morning I was sitting in my kitchen at the Mountain House having breakfast with my husband. Suddenly, out of the corner of my eye, I saw three men approaching from the driveway. They were dressed in all black with hoods covering their heads, and each carried something long and black. I went into complete terror and started planning ways to run and escape. I was almost paralyzed with fear, for in that moment, I was convinced these three menacing-looking men were walking toward us carrying large guns.

As the men neared the house, the reality of the situation presented itself. These were not murderers coming to get me, but the nice guys who cut the yard, walking around with their leaf blowers. While this may seem funny, it was actually terribly upsetting. What upset me most was that, because of the gun violence in my country, I instantly assumed the worst.

Because of the gun control issues in the United States, I walk through life with an unconscious fear that at any moment someone will show up with a gun. This is a real fear that many people can relate to.

Later that week there was news about yet another mass shooting in California, and the statistics presented by the news media were staggering. There have been mass shootings every day since the Sandy Hook tragedy. Our chances of being killed by another American with a gun far outweigh any chance of being killed in a terrorist attack. As I watched a news report, I started to get very angry. I began to feel a strong need to fight back, speak up, and be heard. So I took my rage and anger to the Internet. I posted a picture of a gun with a ban sign across it. The comment said, "Sending prayers to our country. This has to stop!" Within minutes there were hundreds of comments. To my surprise there were women on my page defending their guns. There were comments like, "I'm disappointed in you, Gabby. I need my gun to protect my family."

These comments sent me into a rage. I started preaching to my husband about how insane I thought these responses were. And that the need for guns as "protection" only perpetuated the problem. I said to my husband, "I'm going to post again!" Then my husband responded with some necessary wisdom. "How is that going to help?" he asked. "Your negative post is only going to fuel the fire. Aren't you all about facing adversity with love?" In that moment my husband was my guru. Zach has always been a powerful mirror for me to see my shadow and bring it to the light. Sometimes it's the people closest to us who can reflect back our greatest learning opportunities for spiritual growth. I smiled and said, "You're right. I cannot defend against this fear with anger; I must be an instrument for love."

I refrained from defending, commenting, or deleting the negative comments. Instead I sat with my feelings and called on love. I recognized myself in the angry mothers on my Facebook page. Their need for guns arose from the same sense of fear I had. After all, we are all scared of violence and have the deep desire to protect our families. With compassion I could see their opinions with love.

Gun violence is one of the many horrific issues we're currently facing as a nation. How do we find safety in the midst of uncertainty? How do we find power when we feel so powerless? How do we find peace when there is so much fear?

The answer is to lead from a place of love. Our capacity to tune in to the energy of love gives us the words we need when we're ready to speak up, the compassion we need when it's time to forgive and the power we need when we are lost. As a spiritual activist, I believe that the greatest power we have to combat the terror of these times is our power to live in love. Love casts out all fear.

Every chapter of this book has been leading you to this point. You now know how powerful you truly are. You know that you have the capacity to connect with the force of the Universe to influence others with your presence. You know your power lies in your capacity to be love and spread light.

The more love you bring to the world the more you will inspire others to live in love. Then they will do the same. This ripple effect of love is what changes patterns, creates peaceful revolutions, and ends wars. You may feel that your power is lost in the hands of some insane CEO, terrorist, or fear-based world leader. It's not. Your power lies in your capacity to spread love.

It may be hard to grasp the idea that spreading love can abolish terrorism, reduce gun violence, heal the environment, feed the hungry, free the enslaved, and so on. I get it. I too feel defeated, powerless, and lost a lot of the time. But in the moments when I remember my power lies in my capacity to spread love, I regain my strength, certainty, and peace. We absolutely must commit to this truth in order to save the world.

We change the world when we shift spiritually—when our attitudes become more loving, when we forgive, when we heal our wounds from the past, and when we embrace the present moment. The miracles that occur on an individual level have a massive impact on the collective field of energy. One person's shift toward love shines light onto all.

I write these books to have an impact on your life so that you can have an impact on the world. As each individual lights up his or her life, the world becomes brighter. In our light that darkness cannot co-exist.

When I was in the process of writing this book, I told a literary mentor what it was about. I said, "This book is about helping people find safety in the midst of uncertainty, power when they feel powerless, and love in a fearful world." He replied, "That's lovely and powerful, but books about saving the world don't sell." As a marketer I totally understood where he was coming from. But as a woman living during these difficult times, I was unwilling to give up my intention. While I want all my readers to learn how to manifest their desires, thrive in their careers, and enjoy wildly incredible relationships, what I want most from you is to be the light.

My commitment in this lifetime is to wake up as many people as possible to their power to lead from a place of love. I perceive myself as a can opener who is here to crack you open to your highest potential to serve the world with your joy. I am deeply devoted to waking you up to your true purpose: be love and spread love. Our lives depend on it. These words can no longer be cute buzz phrases that we post on Instagram. These words must be our mission. The safety and security we long for lie in our commitment to love.

The final steps of this book will guide you to embrace your capacity to join me as a spiritual activist. This work will remind you that your connection to the Universe must be used for the highest purpose: to save the world. Follow these steps, and accept my invitation.

Join me in being the light.

Step 1: Wake up.

I have the privilege of witnessing thousands of people embrace their spiritual natures. It's incredible to see people wake up to their connection to love. But far too often, I also see that these spiritually conscious people are extremely unconscious about what's going on in the world. Or maybe they're aware because they watch the news and read the paper, but they are apathetic to the issues. There's nothing more upsetting to me than highly spiritual people who are disengaged from the world around them.

While I do not recommend getting sucked into the dramas of the news, I feel it is our responsibility to consciously wake up to what's going on around us. If we ignore what's happening, we'll fall into the trap of apathy and forget the importance of our light. Being conscious of the darkness in the world fuels our desire to bring more light. Consciousness inspires us to speak up when it's necessary and devote our prayers to those who need them most. Consciousness connects us to all the souls throughout the world who do not have the priv-ileges we may have. Consciousness reminds us to be grateful, joyful, and kind.

Without this consciousness it's easy to get caught up in the littleness of our lives. The insane and ridicu-lous stories we make up, the silly problems we focus on, which can make us very selfish.

If you do identify in any way with being apathetic or unconscious, forgive yourself immediately. Remember that in an instant you can dissolve the patterns of your past and step into the power of this present moment. Right now, make the commitment to shift your focus from your littleness and to the world around you.

Take time each day to pay attention to what's hap-pening in the world, and devote your loving thoughts and prayers to those who need you most.

Step 2: Remember where your true power lies.

Be mindful of the power you call on to create change. Are you an angry peace activist or a lightworker? Know the difference. Become conscious of how you may use fear as power and separation as a weapon. When we become more conscious of what's happening in the world, it's easy to get scared and angry, much like what happened when I got so fiercely outraged by the gun vio-lence in my country. It's okay to get mad, and it's natural to rage, but remember that anger is not where your true power lies. The key to our power is our capacity to lead from a place of love.

So feel the anger, and share your outrage with a friend. Honor your anger and fear as great teachers on the path back to peace. Then, as quickly as possible, return to love. Reconnect to your power through prayer.

Here's a prayer you can use when you need to access your true power:

"I recognize my anger and I honor my reaction to the darkness. I know my true power lies in my capacity to be the light. I call on the energy and thoughts of love to pour through me and inspire me to take action from a place of true power."

Accept your role as a spiritual activist who shows up for the fears of the world with love. Lead from a place of forgiveness and compassion. Know that you can speak up, rise up, and show up with grace. You have the power to dissolve all boundaries with love.

Step 3: The peace of love is shining in you now.

Lesson 188 from *A Course in Miracles* says, "Why wait for Heaven? Those who seek the light are merely covering their eyes. The light is in them now. Enlightenment is but a recognition, not a change at all."

Do you think you need to change your circumstances to change your life? All you need to do is change your mind and remember love. Accept the light within you, and you'll light up the world. Believe in this light no matter what. Your conviction and certainty help others remember their own. Your remembrance alone has the power to heal.

Accept the love that shines through you now. Declare your commitment to live in the light. Honor the wounds that got you here. The Sufi poet Rumi said, "The wound is the place where the light enters you." Trust that your wounds are exactly as the Universe planned. They were divinely placed in your life in the perfect order so that you could show up for them with love and remember the light within. As difficult as your circumstances may have been, take a moment to honor them now. Honor the trauma, honor the pain, and honor the fear, knowing that all along the peace of love was always shining through you. No matter what happens to you in this lifetime, this truth will never change. The peace of love will never leave you.

When the fears of the world take you out, return to the present moment and remember that the peace of love still shines in you now. Gently witness the stories and fearful thoughts as distractions from this truth. In the present moment, you can return to love and be at peace. In the present moment, you can restore your connection to the Universe and release yourself from all suffering.

Step 4: Become an instrument for love.

There is no greater experience than allowing the presence of love to move through you. As you heal your own life through your connection to love, you will be guided to help others do the same. Sometimes that guidance will lead you in directions you never could have imagined. The direction may not always seem logical, but the call will be undeniable.

Throughout my life I've witnessed many transformational leaders follow that undeniable call. One example is Oprah Winfrey. I had the privilege of being invited to a screening of Oprah's OWN series *Belief*. The show featured stunning stories about religions and spiritual practices from around the world, and each story evidenced the power of the universal energy of love. The stories released all religious and spiritual separation and presented us with a vision of what true oneness is.

At the screening, Oprah shared the story behind why she created *Belief*. She said that in her prayers she asked

God to use her for the highest good, and the response she received was to create this series. She put her own money, time, and energy into creating it. At the end of her speech, she teared up as she shared her gratitude for allowing the universal energy of love to work through her in the creation of something so transformational.

We all have the capacity to allow the universal energy of love to use us for the highest good. That is why we are here: to remember love and allow it to move through us, heal us, and inspire us to serve. When we surrender to this commitment, we can truly co-create with the Universe. We can create movements far beyond our logical mind's capacity to see. We can help others heal and serve people all over the world. The simple act of asking, "How would you use me?" opens the floodgates for love to transcend all doubt and limitation. Your fear cannot co-exist in the presence of this love.

That is the final step of this book: become an instrument for the love of the Universe.

Begin each day with this simple prayer:

"How would you use me?"

Then step back and allow. Let love direct your life.

The *Course* says, "You are at peace and you bring peace with you wherever you are." Allowing the Universe to guide you, heal you, and direct you brings that peace back into your consciousness. Peace and love can never be lost.

When you lead your life with grace and love, you begin to feel a swell of energy move through you. You're given words when you don't have them. You're given strength when you are down. You're given synchronicity and support when you feel lost. You're given safety when you're uncertain.

As I conclude this book, I am days away from celebrating 10 years of sober recovery. This anniversary marks the day that I returned to love, the day that I surrendered to the Universe for help. I am in awe of the gifts I have received as the result of allowing the Universe to be my guide. I am in awe of how I have allowed love to work through me. I am in awe of the transformation I have undergone. I am deeply moved by the support, love, and guidance I have grown to rely on. Most important, I am proud of my willingness to heal the world through love. I think about where I was 10 years ago: 25 years old, strung out on drugs, and severely insecure. I was a girl who lived in fear, doubt, and uncertainty. Today I am a woman who lives in the light.

My transformation is yours. It's available to you now. All you have to do is choose love, spread light, and know that the Universe has your back.

ACKNOWLEDGMENTS

There are many incredible people who helped me bring this book to life. My literary mentor, guide, and agent, Michele Martin, who's been on this journey with me from the very beginning. I am deeply grateful for my powerhouse publishers at Hay House. Reid Tracy, Patty Gift, Richelle Fredson, Michelle Pilley, Leon Nacson, Louise Hay, and the entire Hay House family. Big love goes out to my PR team at Sarah Hall Productions, thank you for spreading the love! Thank you Katie Karlson, you are far more than my editor, you are my dear friend. A huge shout-out to my husband, Zach. Hollywood, you are my forever +1, you are my partner and my best friend. Thank you, Z, for putting your heart and soul into this book.

Finally, I thank you, my reader. It's because of you that I write these books. I am deeply inspired by your willingness to grow, heal, and transcend fear and step into your light. You are my hero. I hope this book feels like a huge hug, holding you tightly and reminding you that The Universe Has Your Back!

ABOUT THE AUTHOR

Gabrielle Bernstein is the #1 *New York Times* best-selling author of *The Universe Has Your Back* and has written five additional bestsellers. She was featured on Oprah's *SuperSoul Sunday* as "a next-generation thought leader" and the Oprah Winfrey Network chose Gabrielle to be part of the "SuperSoul 100," a dynamic group of 100 trailblazers whose vision and life's work are bringing a higher level of consciousness to the world. *The New York Times* identified her as "a new role model." YouTube named Gabrielle one of 16 YouTube Next Video Bloggers, she was named one of Mashable's 11 Must-Follow Twitter Accounts for Inspiration, and she's featured on the Forbes List of 20 Best Branded Women. She appears regularly on *The Dr. Oz Show* and co-hosted the Guinness World Record largest guided meditation with Deepak Chopra. Additionally, Gabrielle has been featured in media outlets such as *ELLE*, *OWN*, *Kathie Lee & Hoda*, *TODAY*, *Marie Claire*, *Health*, *SELF*, *Women's Health*, *Cosmopolitan*, *The New York Times*, *Glamour*, the covers of *Success* magazine and *Experience Life* magazine, and more. In September 2019 Gabrielle launches her seventh book, entitled *Super Attractor*. For more on Gabrielle's work, visit GabbyBernstein.com.

Read on for a preview
of Gabrielle Bernstein's

SUPER
ATTRACTOR

Coming in Fall 2019 from Hay House

INTRODUCTION

You Are a Super Attractor

I've always known that there is a nonphysical presence beyond my visible sight. All my life I've intuitively tuned in to it and used it as a source for good. I've tapped into this unlimited presence of power to heal my body, support my relationships, guide my career in the service of others, and attract my greatest desires.

There are many names for this type of spiritual presence. I refer to it interchangeably as the Universe, God, Spirit, inner guidance, love, and other terms too. You may have your own word that resonates with you. Or maybe you're new to spirituality and don't yet have a vocabulary around it. It doesn't matter. What we call it is irrelevant. Connecting to it is imperative. The very fact that you are reading this book right now is evidence that you have listened, consciously or unconsciously, to divine guidance that led you here, and you are willing to claim that connection.

I honor you for your willingness. Claiming my connection to the presence of this power has directed the course of my life. The simple choice to tune in to this source of love has helped me recover from addiction, heal PTSD, undo fearful beliefs, and live with clear purpose. My connection to the presence of love has been my guide, my protector, and my partner in the co-creation of my life. Living my life in daily devotion to this non-physical source of power has made me a Super Attractor.

Being a Super Attractor means that what I believe is what I receive. I can co-create the world I want to see by aligning with good-feeling emotions and directing them toward my desires. I can tap into an unlimited source of creative energy to contribute inspired ideas, offer wisdom, receive abundance, and feel free. And best of all, I can harness this power into a force for good in the world.

Being a Super Attractor doesn't mean I haven't had to face very real challenges. But I can see clearly how my struggles have been part of a bigger plan to help me strengthen my faith in my Super Attractor connection. I've chosen to perceive hard life experiences as spiritual assignments for growth and healing. I've accepted that nothing happens by accident. And I know that as long as I remember I'm a Super Attractor, I will be able to accept difficult experiences as opportunities to fine-tune my inner power and get closer to consciousness. The tough stuff offers me a chance to shine the crystal that is me. Being a Super Attractor doesn't mean everything is perfect—but it does mean that I show up for life with faith, no matter what. Claiming my Super Attractor power has helped me to move through rough times with much more grace, honesty, and compassion than I otherwise would.

Living my life in this way has brought me what I desire most: freedom. I feel free knowing that there is an ever-present energy of love within me and around me. I'm free knowing that I'm always being guided and that I have the power to co-create the world I want to see. Freedom is the greatest gift of all. Nothing holds me back. I no longer play small. For more than a decade, I've lived, loved, and taught with this freedom. Freedom has given me the experience of being an untethered force of light in the world.

As a spiritual teacher, I have witnessed hundreds of thousands of people throughout the world begin to wake up to the presence of freedom within. I see these transformations daily. But while that awakening is beautiful, it isn't enough. Too often we treat it as the end point, when it's really just the beginning. We may know that we can feel better and therefore attract more, but we must go further and fully embody that truth in order to be free. Embodying this truth begins by undoing the belief systems of fear that block us from being Super Attractors. We must be willing and committed to change the way we think, act, and live.

In my case, I didn't have to go out and find this connection; I just had to slow down and remember it. I've devoted my life to the process of slowing down and realigning with the presence of inner power. With each meditation, I vibrate at a higher frequency; with each prayer, I surrender to a power greater than myself. My dedication to the spiritual realm has given me the freedom I desire. I am not exceptional. You have this connection too, and claiming it is both fun and easy. In this book, I want to share with you how to connect to that power.

You may be wondering what I mean when I talk about freedom. When you align yourself with your Super Attractor energy, you no longer feel blocked by fear. You remember that you are a spirit having a human experience. The spirit within you is the presence of inspiration, joy, and the truth of who you are. When you practice these steps, you remember that you are a wise, powerful, healthy, and holy spirit. When you accept this, you can be free. The feeling of freedom is inevitable when you attune your energy with the presence of your truth. You may not stay connected to this truth all the time, but the more often you turn to it, the easier it will be to feel free.

I want you to know this: You are a Super Attractor.

If that feels strange to you right now, that's okay. But I know that by the time you finish this book, you will claim that power with total confidence and ease. You will know beyond a shadow of a doubt that you are a Super Attractor.

In 2016, I published a book called *The Universe Has Your Back: Transform Fear to Faith*. Readers throughout the world followed the book's lessons to strengthen their faith in the Universe. They reclaimed their connection to a higher power and restored their faith in love. When I was preparing to write a new book, I intuitively knew that it was time to take these teachings to the next level. This book is that next step. With the practices outlined in the coming chapters, I'm going to push the spiritual envelope to teach you how to fine-tune your spiritual connection to effortlessly attract what you want into your life. If you haven't read *The Universe Has Your Back*, don't sweat it. It's not a prerequisite. Trust that you were guided here first for a reason.

You may already be on a spiritual path. You may already practice manifesting and live by the Law of Attraction. Or these concepts may be completely new to you. Either way, this book will help them become second nature. Throughout the book I will share my own personal methods for aligning with your Super Attractor presence. Some of these practices have been greatly influenced by my teachers Abraham-Hicks, Dr. Wayne W. Dyer, Yogi Bhajan, and the metaphysical text *A Course in Miracles*. But my greatest teacher of all has been my life experience. Each day offers new opportunities to get closer to the Universe and strengthen my Super

Attractor power. Each life challenge offers new miracles and lessons. Throughout the book I'll call on my own personal examples of what it's like to live in alignment and be a Super Attractor.

Reclaiming Your Super Attractor Power

To master your Super Attractor power, you must start by understanding how you've likely become disconnected from it. In nearly 15 years as a spiritual teacher, I've gained a very clear understanding of the common ways people misuse and block this power. I expect you'll recognize yourself in some (or all) of the most common types.

Did you forget your power?

Even a person on a spiritual path can forget that they're a Super Attractor. It's all too easy to get sucked into the fear-based stories of the world and weaken your faith. When fear takes over, you go into a kind of comatose state. You literally forget who you really are. You build up belief systems of separation, lack, judgment, and negativity. All these false perceptions deny your inner power and block your Super Attractor power. This book will be a wake-up call to remind you of who you really are. Just by opening to this introduction, you've begun to wake up and remember.

Are you manic manifesting?

There are many people who read personal growth books, attend seminars, meditate, pray . . . and still feel stuck. I hear this often: "Gabby, I'm doing everything right, but I still feel so off. I'm praying, meditating, and using positive affirmations, but I'm still not attracting what I want. What's wrong?!"

What's wrong is that they are doing what I call manic manifesting. These folks have faith in the Universe, and lots of spiritual tools, but they are energetically blocking their connection. They've been playing tricks with the Universe rather than aligning with their true power. Manic manifesting happens when someone has all the spiritual tools and jargon but forgets the most important part of attracting: to tune in to the Universe. You can say affirmations, pray, and meditate every day, and still not attract because your energy is out of alignment. Instead of allowing yourself to receive, you want to "get." This book will teach you that the most important element of manifesting with the Universe is to embody the energy of love. If you identify as a manic manifester, you're in the right place! In this book I'll hook you up with a whole new way of being.

Are you a pusher?

A pusher is someone who tries to push and control to reach their goals and feel safe. They believe that the more they do, the more they'll achieve. They're trying to "make things happen" rather than allowing themselves to attract naturally. This is a common characteristic, and it's one that many cultures often seem to reward. Pushers have a fear-based belief that if they're not super productive, nothing will happen for them. Little do they know that their pushy energy is blocking their capacity to attract! The Universe doesn't respond as well to frantic energy. Rather, the Universe vibrates at a positive frequency, and to co-create with it your energy must align.

The practices in this book will help you slow down, be still, and allow. I will teach you the art of allowing so that you can stop pushing, feel secure, and start receiving naturally.

Does fear have you in a headlock?

Each day brings new opportunities to lean toward fear or lean into love. While we always have a choice, we often (quite unconsciously) default to fear. We choose fear in many ways, from the TV we watch to the conversations we have to the thoughts we entertain. The presence of fear is a sure sign we've disconnected from the loving presence of the Universe.

Throughout the book I'll offer you practical tools and spiritual principles to undo fear and reclaim love. Undoing fear doesn't have to be hard. In fact, it can be much easier than you ever imagined. Get ready to create radical shifts fast!

Do you judge?

Judging, comparing, attacking, and seeing ourselves as separate from others all disconnect us from the Universe. If you identify as a judgmental person (judging others or yourself), take a moment to acknowledge how it makes you feel. Be honest and gentle with yourself as you do this. While you may feel justified in your judgment or try to rationalize it, it's undeniable how negative it makes you feel. Being a Super Attractor is about feeling good, and in this book I'll give you lots of amazing tools and spiritual practices to help you cultivate joy and have fun! As you become willing to release your judgment and choose compassion and peace instead, you will reconnect to your power.

These are just a few of the common ways we block our Super Attractor power. The good news is that your power never left you! You simply forgot about it. This book will guide you to recognize it, claim it, use it to attract what you want, and be a force for good in the world.

Let me guide you to become a Super Attractor through powerful steps explained in the upcoming chapters. These chapters will include spiritual exercises and lessons that build on each other so that by the end you will have fully claimed your power. While each step in this book can be applied independently, I've placed them in an order that has a cumulative effect. Practice each lesson as presented so that you can get the most out of this transformational process. You may find that some lessons resonate with you more than others. That's okay! Once you've gone through each chapter, you can then apply the tools interchangeably and at your own pace. Most importantly—have fun! The more fun you have, the stronger your Super Attractor power becomes. Fun turns you into a magnet for miracles.

And here's the promise: When you accept that you are a Super Attractor, life gets awesome! You feel joyful, inspired, purposeful, and empowered. You'll no longer feel the need to control, compare, or push, and you'll settle into a sense of ease. Best of all, you'll become a powerful example for others—and you'll vibrate at such a high, loving frequency that your energy will be felt far and wide.

This text will help you to understand the importance of living in alignment with the Universe—not just dabbling in your practice when it feels convenient. I don't want your spiritual life compartmentalized and kept separate from your day-to-day experiences. I want you to live a spiritual life all the time. I want you to feel a sense of awe each day as you witness miracles unfold. I want you to feel connected to a spiritual force that you can rely on. I want you to attract what you desire and create a life filled with purpose, happiness, abundance, and peace. I want you to feel free.

Accepting that you are a Super Attractor will change everything. You'll trust that it's safe to release the past, and you'll no longer fear the future. You'll tap into an infinite source of abundance, energy, joy, and well-being. This well-being will become the norm for you, and you'll grow to embrace it as your birthright. Most importantly, you'll know intuitively how to show up for life and bring more light to the world around you.

This book is a journey of remembering where your true power lies. You'll learn how to co-create the life you want. You'll accept that life can flow, that attracting is fun, and that you don't have to work so hard to get what you want. Most important, you'll feel good.

Becoming a Force of Love in the World

Once you claim your Super Attractor power, the question then becomes, what will you do with it? When you feel good, you give off a presence of joy that can elevate everyone around you. By claiming your true power, you will help others do the same. The practices here will empower you to live your purpose, and they will amplify abundance, happiness, health, and peace for everyone you come into contact with and beyond. By the end of this book, you will have a greater understanding of your higher purpose. You will know how to fulfill your function: to be a force of love in the world.

It's time to claim your power. Turn to Chapter 1 and let's begin.

We hope you enjoyed this Hay House book. If you'd like to receive our online catalog featuring additional information on Hay House books and products, or if you'd like to find out more about the Hay Foundation, please contact:

Hay House, Inc., P.O. Box 5100, Carlsbad, CA 92018-5100
(760) 431-7695 or (800) 654-5126
(760) 431-6948 (fax) or (800) 650-5115 (fax)
www.hayhouse.com® • www.hayfoundation.org

Published in Australia by:
Hay House Australia Pty. Ltd., 18/36 Ralph St.,
Alexandria NSW 2015 • *Phone:* 612-9669-4299 • *Fax:* 612-9669-4144
www.hayhouse.com.au

Published in the United Kingdom by:
Hay House UK, Ltd., Astley House, 33 Notting Hill Gate,
London W11 3JQ • *Phone:* 44-20-3675-2450 • *Fax:* 44-20-3675-2451
www.hayhouse.co.uk

Published in India by: Hay House Publishers India,
Muskaan Complex, Plot No. 3, B-2, Vasant Kunj, New Delhi 110 070
Phone: 91-11-4176-1620 • *Fax:* 91-11-4176-1630
www.hayhouse.co.in

Access New Knowledge.
Anytime. Anywhere.

Learn and evolve at your own pace
with the world's leading experts.

www.hayhouseU.com

MORE RESOURCES FROM

GABRIELLE BERNSTEIN

THE UNIVERSE HAS YOUR BACK JOURNAL

In the pages of this beautiful writing journal, you'll find inspiring quotes drawn from Gabrielle Bernstein's core teaching of trusting the universe, along with gorgeous artwork designed to spark your own journaling experience of creativity and connection.